T0273949

EMBODY YOUR EGO

THE ART AND SCIENCE OF HACKING THE MATRIX

An easy and practical guide to incarnate our human technology

CINDY BARASCOUT

TABLE OF CONTENTS

CHAPTER 1

What Magic Is and Is Not

Many people have different perspectives of magic, and associate it with something sinful or alien to this world. In the collective imagination, stories around magic arise from patriarchal institutions based on the western conception of magic, rooted in ancient Judeo-Christian and Greco-Roman heritage, and continuing through European colonial exploration in the 16th century.

The Christian view of magic was a mixture of beliefs from the Babylonians, Persians, and Egyptians, distinct from proper religion. Because of that, believers felt magic — and practitioners of magic — needed to be exterminated because such ideas and practices were against God's will.

The word *magic* comes from the Persian magus, meaning chemistry. In Arabic, one who makes chemistry is an Alchemist.

Al = the one

Chemistre = chemistry

So *magus* or magician is the one who does *chemistry* with reality. Today, chemistry is associated with science: a logical practice that understands everything through analysis of an object, separate from the being. But the alchemist and magus analyze things by *becoming* those things. In order to understand water, the alchemist becomes water. To

1

understand fire, the alchemist becomes the fire. It isn't external, but internal.

Because once you place yourself as something aside, you will never know it. You can only believe it as something else, but not really know it because you haven't collapsed the separation between you and that thing. But by becoming it, you know it, and that is the way to know anything.

The reason we separate magic from our essential nature is that in the past when an alchemist was doing something, people would make a circle and watch, and the act of looking made them think they were seeing magic, but not being part of it.

In Latin, the act of staring at something in a focused way means *miracle*. The *magus* used to do these kinds of miracles that people didn't understand, though they stared at it. This created the idea of separation, or something happening outside myself that I don't get, so it's not part of myself. Until you become the experience itself, you can't fully understand it.

It comes down to a question of belief. But to believe something does not make it true. The miracle is you witnessing what happens and that is what makes you part of it.

But the practice and science behind the act of doing magic are as natural as breathing. Magic is, in fact, a human right, arising from a natural and anciently known capacity.

Beliefs around magic have divided humanity to the point where we have killed each other over whether we believe in the universal forces through religion or our individuality. Confusion and fear around the hunting and killing of magicians and wise women have created wars, persecutions, and, as a consequence, a disconnection from our true selves.

I believe magic is something bigger than what separates us as humans. Magic unites us all. Our beliefs around magic — not magic itself — create fear and separation. Looking back in history we find magical patterns and practices everywhere. We've always used magic, even if it hasn't always been called magic.

I would define magic as the ability to conduct the inner power that comes from the Source, channeled through our bodies, and building matter through the mind.

Magic has such power that people who have practiced and publicly shared their explorations and findings to help humanity — through inventions, new ways of doing things, healing, or simply thinking — have been labeled inadequate and dangerous.

Stories created fear about exploring different dimensions within us, considering any type of magic, so-called, as black magic. Magic is more than black and white. Doing good or ill is part of our free will. We choose what we do, regardless of magic. If you truly believe that what you do to your brother or sister, you do to yourself, then whatever you live for — whether or not it's considered magic — will have the same constructive or destructive effect. These fear-based beliefs in human inner powers have caused a deep disassociation between our inner world and our supernatural capacities. As a result we ignore and fear a great part of ourselves — our connection to the Source, or God.

Believing that God is someone or something foreign to ourselves has placed us in a place of fear, confusion, and low vibration. We are slowly coming to our senses, however, understanding our authentic relationship with ourselves, with our essence, which is love — love being God and everything from what this world and the beings in this world have been created.

A Relationship with the Spiritual World

When I started questioning many things that I had acquired through my upbringing in Guatemala, I realized that I wanted to explore my own relationship with the spiritual world, where the force of everything comes from and is sustained.

I grew up in an environment where personal empowerment was not practiced, let alone understood. I was raised in a conservative religion. I didn't find my own spirituality there, and I knew little about other spiritual practices. This church did not work for me. It was, above all, based on guilt and fear. As a nonheterosexual woman, I had to accept that I was never going to be a part of this community by being who I was. I decided to stop judging and feeling guilty, and I

3

stepped out of my ordinary world for an adventure.

I wanted to experience life from a deeper state of being, not through the common and social ways life was represented. I started to open my mind and to look for paths that would resonate more with me.

In 2011, I began to study Journalism in Buenos Aires, Argentina. I knew I wanted to write, research, and go on adventures. I now consider myself a spiritual journalist, with a deep passion and respect for truth. I use my journalistic talents to communicate concepts from higher planes to the physical reality.

I started practicing yoga and meditation in a tantric school in Palermo, Buenos Aires. Yoga led me to plant medicine practices, and then to many amazing and powerful things that I now consider my strongest resources because they guided me into understanding who I am.

Some 14 years later, this book reflects my understanding about my inner powers, the way I perceive magic, and how it has changed my life. It's also a way for me to share my journey and my process with others.

I now understand and recognize the Source within me, how to feel and be happy and free, without needing anything but myself. After years of feeling guilty for being who I am, letting down people around me, and playing victim because the world seemed so cruel and I felt misunderstood, I started to ask myself what I was doing to create an amazing life for myself. I wondered if I'd be stuck forever in the same old sad story. I realized I could choose to emerge from victimhood and decide to live.

As long as my actions did not affect other people's freedom, I could use my time and energy to create a magical life for me and my wildest dreams.

I freely and openly practice my magical powers, or my yogic mental powers — applying the laws of metaphysics, my free will, and the elixir of wisdom from my past experience, toward an amazing future that I decided to believe awaits me, because I can feel it now. This has made me the most powerful and freest version of myself.

Once I felt and knew that I was different from other people, I began to think that my differences from others were worth exploring. I didn't know then that this would allow me to create something for myself rather than rely on what others have created.

An Exercise

Have you ever questioned your inner powers? Have you ever questioned what magic means to you, and only you? How would you explain magic to a little kid without repeating something that you have been told, but, instead, expressing what you feel magic to be? To help you with that, try this:

Write a list of your current beliefs and thoughts about this magic.

Circle the ones that don't belong to you or don't resonate with you. For example, what have you been told is magic at school, in your family, as a society?

Unlearning what we already know sometimes is more important than learning new things. It is about needing less and not adding more.

When you question your concept of magic and that of your personal power, you will start to discover your truth and start acting on it.

Alternate Paths to Exploring Yourself

I started practicing yoga, meditation, and exploring the plant medicine world over a period of 14 years, and I continue to practice yoga today.

I didn't choose to move on with business school in the most privileged university in Guatemala, but to explore my writing and sexuality where I could do it freely and openly, without feeling guilty or ashamed. At the age of 21, I began to unlearn what I'd been learning all my life. I left my country and the people around me. I had already felt an attraction to yoga, but I didn't expect to fall in love with it as I did. For me, this meant a connection with my mind, emotions, body, and spirituality, which gave me access to everything that I was really looking for. My committed practice of yoga began then.

If you don't know where to start, but are curious about understanding your relationship with magic, you can do the following:

- Open your mind into moving to a different place or country. Sometimes our dreams and our personality go beyond the physical place where we grow, and new horizons always mean new relationships, new perspectives, and new self-knowledge. And even if this is not a must, space and time away from our known world helps bring clarity and answers to important questions.

- Be brave in going against the mainstream. I changed from studying business to investigative journalism and creative writing in college. In my country, Guatemala, people don't necessarily respect this because being a journalist is associated with dirty politics and being hunted when exposing the truth. Being an author is associated with being an artist, but the belief at that time was that only a few artists in Guatemala actually make a living out of it. I chose to go somewhere unknown and unpredictable.

- Seek support in virtual or other communities. I started looking and tried different yoga studios, until I found the right one at the right moment, with people who inspired me and who allowed me to explore myself.

By opening myself to the world, I found what resonated with my authentic self. Through different experiences that placed me outside my comfort zone, I learned who I was not, which would lead me eventually to learn about who I actually was.

But I still had not healed my deepest wounds, and I was hurting. I was enjoying sex and a partnership where I could freely express love and learn who I was as a partner, but suddenly alcohol and drugs came into my life. I thought it was great. I tried LSD and MDMA, and I understood many, many things, but my emotional body was deeply unbalanced. What started out to be fun, turned unstable. I was insecure, I needed to feel my emotions, but I didn't want to: I was codependent in my relationship, and started to be jealous and angry.

So that new character — being a lesbian journalist yogi in Buenos Aires — didn't last long. Our relationship ended in one of the most painful experiences I ever had. Luckily, my yoga practice and my silent pilgrimage to Santiago de Compostela helped clear my mind so I could acquire the strength to navigate this tragedy. I had to let go, and accept, to create a space to heal myself deeper. I later realized that my life had changed, and I could look back and be thankful that I was no longer in a toxic relationship. This was my first spiritual degree. Through every heartbreak I have grown stronger and wiser.

I still didn't know what challenges life was going to throw at me. I now understand that these experiences were inevitable and reflected my inner world. I learned the hard way that drugs and distractions were not a good idea. They created more pain and confusion inside me.

Socrates, one of the wisest men and best-known philosophers in history, said, "I only know that I don't know anything" – which brings a sense of humility to the idea of being open to exploring life in different ways. A sense of innocence and wonder. A sense of adventure and courage. But wisdom also needs to be practiced.

Magic Is Power; Power Is Magic in Action

I believe that we are meant to find magic.

We are meant to discover who we are by choosing to discover the pathway back home, back to the infinite, back to the ocean itself, back to our own essence, which is the God within and without. Magic becomes obvious not by reading about it, but by living it.

Once we start exploring and feeling the powerful essence that resides within us, the openness and surrender of this feeling will flow through us. Through time we will begin to understand the layers that unfold this essence. Powers, wisdom and higher visions will come to our lives, and we will understand their meanings.

The word *magic* means *the power of influencing the course of events by using supernatural forces; having or apparently having supernatural* powers; to move, change, or create by or as if by magic; having or seeming to have the power to make impossible things happen; miraculous; phenomenal; superhuman; supernatural; and transcendental.

What is common between all of these descriptions is that magic *appears* to happen. In this book, I want to help you understand what magic means *to you*, so you can develop your own authentic relationship with your inner powers, and start creating substantial transformational experiences in your life.

How? By choosing to be courageous. And despite my mistakes, I always asked God to help me to see the truth. This meant questioning and challenging the truth of most people around me. I practiced being silent and simply observing. This led me to spending time by myself, traveling to different countries, and exploring who I was, without expectation.

I had to go through darkness, disrespect myself, learn about setting boundaries and loving myself. I took a leap of faith into the unknown. I have since written five books, and I live in a place where I can be myself. I have created an amazing life.

Choosing to Discover the Divinity Within

Magic is about being who you are and choosing to discover your God within — your essence. You are power itself. You are a magician and a fool at the same time. You know everything and nothing. This is the paradox of life.

Believe in your higher self and be courageous about it.

How can you actually use your magic as your higher self? The following steps may help you put your inner magician into practice:

1) Find a space and time to explore who you are. This could mean making space and time for journaling, reading, going to retreats, participating in book clubs, taking in art expositions, or any activity that requires self exploration.

2) Expose yourself to different contexts, circles, and experiences that can help you get to know yourself. It can be as small as taking a different path to work, because this is how you will start moving

everything else. What feels right or wrong are cues that will teach you about yourself.

3) If possible, travel by yourself and place yourself out of your comfort zone, which will show you how to treat yourself and the people you enjoy being near.

4) The more you know about yourself, the more you can understand yourself.

The first decision is as simple as taking the time and space to explore your inner space and question your learning, your beliefs about things and mental concepts, connecting with your feelings — then you will find your own truth, your own dreams, and your own way.

I had to question truths and expectations from everyone: my mom's, my dad's, and my oldest friends. As a nonheterosexual person in my community and country, I was taught that I was sinful. That I should feel guilt and regret and look for healing because I was probably sick. But that didn't feel right, so I chose to trust in myself and encourage who I was even if I disappointed everyone around me, especially my family.

This came with a gift. Because I had to question everything else, I got to know and give life to my authentic self.

How to know your authentic self? Here are some steps:

1. Question what truths are really yours, and trust that feeling. What is really important to you as a human, as a lover, as a professional, as an artist?

2. Even if it seems crazy to you and others (because it is simply different and wild), always trust your feelings and inner compass. It will show you who you are and where you need to be.

3. If you are and feel different, try not to judge yourself or fit in. Shutting your light is the real mistake.

If you follow your heart and gut, you will find freedom and joy in who you are. Trust that you will find the right people, place, and relationships that will liberate and celebrate you instead of judging you. Believe that your light is important in the world, as many other people that were different did, and brought amazing things to humanity. I took my things and left the known world behind.

A Healing Journey

I made a serious choice to spend time by myself. I needed to get away from being told how wrong I was.

After four years in Buenos Aires, I decided to study for my first yoga teacher training, which also offered plant medicine such as cacao, rapé, and mescaline. Training detoxed my body and led me to different states of consciousness that I wasn't aware of: bliss, connection, self- love, lightness, and inspiration. I finally started to experience a state of clarity, harmony, and discernment within me.

If you are going through a healing or transformational process, you can apply the following steps:

1. Find a spiritual practice such as yoga that can help you move the energy inside of you, heal, and understand yourself.

2. Find a creative practice or an artistic discipline that you enjoy that reflects your inner world. Art can work as a channel and give you information about yourself, your current state of mind, what moves you and lights your heart.

3. Put yourself first when you know and feel that you need to go in, instead of being socially active or completely busy. The outer world will always demand your attention, but you need to take time for yourself, to give more to the world when you are more balanced, since you will eventually feel balanced.

4. Take care of your body by having a good amount of sleep, constant exercise, and healthy eating.

If you bring these different practices or habits into your day, they can deeply support your transformation and healing process, because they will keep you centered and balanced.

Healing means also facing our inner darkness, which means being open to making mistakes, setting boundaries, and finding better ways to love yourself. This is a process and consciously choosing to experience the process is key.

Know Your Demons

When I committed to my inner journey, I had to know my demons, too. This meant doing the shadow work, or that which is not yet seen by the consciousness, even if there was resistance.

The same shadow that made me hurt in my first relationships, presented itself in my next one, the following one, and the next one.

By choosing not to see this shadow, life was throwing me the truth in obvious ways. I experienced increasingly painful treason, codependency, and fear. I suffered because I avoided feeling what I needed to feel. I knew I had to go deeper. I decided to experience my first master plant: ayahuasca.

Healing is like going through a dark cave, so keep these next steps in mind:

1. Choosing healing is not comfortable or necessarily joyful, but you will get to the other side. Consistency in your practice, which means being committed and disciplined about your priorities, will bring you freedom, wisdom, and eventually even love into what you thought was only darkness.

2. Focus on the outcome rather than what is hurting. Freedom of being conditioned by fears, for example, is a great outcome.

3. Make decisions based on what you feel and need. Pamper yourself, sleep, and surround yourself with people who can listen to or support you.

Healing is a serious choice, but you can have fun with it. There are tools to help you.

Here are some tips you can add to your healing process:

1. Stop pleasing people. Choose pleasing yourself.

2. Putting yourself first is an act of self-love, and you create independence for yourself and others. Nobody should be carrying other people's burdens, even if culturally that is what

is expected of you.

3. Can you think of a situation where you were forced into having faith? What was the outcome? Can you see that by believing in yourself you discovered more of who you were, and how powerful that is?

Doubt comes from Fear — Certainty from Love

If we refuse to accept and understand that we actually have a choice to change and transform our lives, we will always be playing victim, believing that life simply happens to us and we have absolutely no power over it.

I ask myself all the time: Am I choosing to doubt myself, or I am choosing to feel certain of myself and my feelings?

I avoid looking at the media or sustaining gossipy conversations. Television, newspapers, and social media content repeat the same information that makes us feel confused and fearful. This information overload makes us doubt our capacity to connect to our inner creators.

The word *fear* means *an unpleasant emotion caused by the belief that someone or something is dangerous, likely to cause pain, or a threat. Being in fear is a state marked by an anxious concern.*

The word *doubt* means *a feeling of uncertainty or lack of conviction, confidence, and distrust about one's abilities, or other people's.*

So *fear* and *doubt* can be considered equal states of being, one related to the outside world, and the other one to the inner, both feeding themselves. That's because when we are in a state of fear we are not in trust, or in certainty. If we are in a fear state of consciousness, we are going to be conditioned on our decision making due to uncertainty and confusion, and distrust or doubt ourselves and the world.

Fear is equal to doubt, and certainty is equal to love.

Are you choosing doubt or certainty in yourself? Choosing between certainty or doubt will help you know who you are, and what truly feels right for you. Just feel it, right now, to trust in your dreams, to trust your feelings. I think it's in our nature that no one enjoys fear or doubt, because it contracts us, as love and certainty expand us.

Once I started choosing certainty over doubt, even in the most absurd things, I realized I was essentially believing in myself, believing in that piece, a very important piece, the divine piece, within me. This is what I consider magic, to believe in what I am not seeing with my eyes, but feeling with my heart, even if it's absurd for most people, because the senses that experience magic are not the physical ones, but the senses of the heart and soul. But magic, as with everything else, requires practice.

"The world is full of magic things, patiently waiting for our senses to grow sharper."

— W.B Yeats

The more I entered and incarnated this state of certainty within me, the more I realized I didn't need anything. I am already in heaven when I live from my heart, so everything that comes is extra, it is a gift. Being alive and being able to write this book and acknowledge it, is a gift.

Rationally understanding some concepts can help you understand what makes sense. Here is a way to bring magical practicality into your life and understand doubt and certainty:

1. When you doubt yourself, choose certainty.

2. Be aware of your thoughts and separate them between doubt and certainty, so you will know what you are choosing.

3. Remember you are already complete, you are already free. Your decision making can come from curiosity and love.

4. Choose what feels more fun, expansive, and enjoyable.

If you choose love and certainty over fear and doubt, you will create opportunities. Your life will be based on love and, therefore, it will flow back to you as a flow from an infinite river.

Habits for Choosing Love

Choosing love and certainty over fear and doubt is a habit. It's an active meditation for creating a magical life. You can do this with even the most absurd things.

Choosing love and certainty requires practice and consistency. It shouldn't be a one-day thing that you forget before going back to the old business. If you are really committed to becoming the best version of yourself, then practicing being aware of your inner state of being is super important.

The following habits can help you create a structure and optimal environment into the state that you are building:

1. Meditate every day. Closing off your physical senses and tuning in with the nonphysical senses is key to creating a deeper connection with your feelings. Tune to feelings of love, faith, success, freedom, and certainty.

2. Wake up, sit on your bed, close your eyes, take deep breaths and feel the feeling of certainty that your day will, and already is, bringing you amazing things, opportunities, and the right challenges to become and polish your developing into your highest potential.

3. Anchor the feeling of success, peace, love, etc by feeling it and sustaining it in your body, all the way down to your tailbone and back to your heart and vision. Whatever it is, you are that in that moment, so the more and more you feel it physically, the more real it feels and becomes.

If you start incorporating what you know you deserve, then you will start creating and attracting this new reality in your life. Believing that you can create something out of nowhere is magic, because essentially you are already believing in what you are not seeing. You are always creating.

Magic is just a science that we don´t understand yet.

— *Arthur C. Clarke.*

Starting to practice your creative powers is the beginning to solidify and fortify them, as we do with any other muscle. Once we have built faith around ourselves, we start creating what seems bigger and bigger things, if that is what we are choosing. Recognize yourself as a creator and know that you are creating the experiences you live.

My decision on this life, and what brings me peace and joy, is to perceive it as a reality game. Life is, from the human skin to my insides, free will, and I am using my free will to perceive the outside like that. I do know that I don't hold the infinite truth, and probably we are not meant to, so whether it is truly a game reality or not, it doesn't really matter. It works for me. Because by being that contemplative observer behind the explorer, I have worked my way to recognizing who I am and how to work through my human avatar.

My hope is that once you know that you are free to choose your higher vision and feel it with your body, your full potential will start to awaken and, therefore, the reality game around you will start shifting according to your new choices.

CHAPTER 2

The New Age Era

The New Age era constitutes a range of spiritual, religious, medicinal behaviors, and beliefs that emerged during the 1970s in Western society. A lot of it was considered to be esoteric and pagan.

The term *esoteric* means *secret or occult practices that look to unify mind, the body, and the spirit through alternative ways rather than the church ways*. The so-called New Age movement was composed of different phenomena, such as the counterculture of the 1960s as expressed in music, art, self-exploration, psychedelics, spiritual practices, and UFO theories, and it has now expanded around the world. Certain New Age beliefs have always existed in ancient cultures and civilizations such as in India, Africa, Australia, America and certain northern European countries such as Sweden. So, new or old is basically the same in essence, but different because it is perceived differently.

In the 15th century, in the early stages of world expansion, Europeans interpreted the cultures they encountered through the framework of the dominant Roman Catholic culture. They saw indigenous peoples as resources to be exploited, as well as souls to be saved and converted to Christianity.

With the rise of scientific anthropology in the 18th and 19th centuries, Europeans began to distinguish themselves from indigenous peoples by claiming they possessed a rational and more evolved intelligence that they lacked. For the Europeans, the continuity of the non-rational indigenous practices seemed unknown and dark. The practices of the native cultures of Africa, Asia, and the Americas came to be regarded as evidence of a failure among indigenous peoples to achieve a stage of rational development, which was considered inferior in contrast to the one achieved by the colonizers of America. Modern science evolved from the essence of magical practices, the ancient sciences of nature. Some rational practices remained, while others were neglected. Although referred to by different names, magical practices were essentially practices that worked with the natural forces of nature.

Ancient civilizations had been working and studying for thousands of years with the cycles of the stars, the cycles of crops, the cycles of the human body, reading and expecting the influences of the planets due to the patterns and cycles and the influence of the sky and stars in human, animal, and plant life. They had experience and understood about inducing and accessing different altered states of consciousness through plant medicine, meditation, breath, and repetition of words that evoked feelings or vibrations. As in ancient Greece and ancient Egypt, the use of symbols that contained and concentrated specific energy to attain specific kinds of powers, was never something random. It was considered to be knowledge of the self, the body, the mind, and the way to connect and be the spirit.

In Western thinking anything that wasn't rational was considered dangerous. But these ideas and practices never ceased to exist, because they involve something as natural as breathing.

People love labeling things. People are used to judging everything, from the subtle to the dense. It sometimes seems that this is the only way we know how to live and move. One of the most powerful meditative practices we can learn to apply as individuals is practice being nonjudgmental, because it separates things and what's more it separates you from that.

When Magic Was Also Science

Before esoteric practices were seen as wrong, pagans were those people beyond the borders of the kingdoms, who had grown from generations in that land, and since they applied their own healing, harvesting, and spiritual practices, they were independent from the kingdom's laws. They were considered a threat since they were not supporting the system. This is where the word paganism comes from, and then associated with witchcraft and black magic.

Alchemists, prophets, and scientific thinkers including Galileo Galilei, Jesus, Plato, Socrates, and Nicolás Copernicus, were considered fools and enemies of the Church and the people, and were hunted, executed, or rejected. But now, as the veils between technology, science, metaphysics and spirituality lift, more people are starting to see that even if some practices are not scientifically founded, there is nevertheless truth in them. That's because the particle of God or the source of everything cannot be measured or studied by human tools, because they transcend our human mind.

Today many are studying and questioning our relationship with this Source, which is vital to understand who we are. This is what some people call the New Age, and what a lot of people are starting to read and learn. The science behind the law of attraction, the laws of the universe, the chakras or yoga science, currents not availed by conservative or conventional scientists, have always been present and part of who we are. Our bodies are the real technology, and everything that we do is to improve the signal of our technology. We don't need anything from outside, but simply to solidify and understand the interconnections we already have within.

I started to apply my findings into my practice to explore, understand, and prove to myself my own relationship to the Source. Now I create and attract the experiences that my heart longs for and I no longer worry. I focus on becoming what I now know I am: complete, happy, grateful, powerful, abundant, and open to receive. It is a state of mind, it is a state of being, such as the law of mentality expressed in the laws of the universe, from the forgotten books from the teachings of the Egyptian Hermes Trismegistus.

If we knew we were energy, then we would be more careful and aware of the thinking that we are choosing. That is why reading and understanding laws around energy, and how they work, helped me go deeper into my mind and the power of my thinking and inner potential.

19

Let's look at your own relationship with your inner powers using the following points:

1. In your journal, draw two columns.

2. Make a list of all your everyday thoughts on the left column, and circle the ones that are more repetitive during your day.

3. In the right column write thoughts that are coherent with your higher potential self. Notice the difference of some thoughts from those in the left column. For example, you can see on the left column some thoughts like: I am not good enough or work is hard. But from your higher truth on the right column, you have now changed them to: I deserve an amazing life, making money is easy and fun, unconditional love exists.

4. You change your life by choosing the thoughts that are coherent with what you want.

5. Thoughts that trigger your emotions are the strongest ones and also have something punctual to teach you. (You can also train yourself to create emotions, which we will address further in this book.) Make a separate column on thoughts that create emotions in your body. For example: Thinking about a job you lost makes you angry or feel failure, while thinking about a recognition from the past makes you feel proud and successful.

6. These thoughts that create emotion in your body have more impact in your creative process (expansive or contractive) and probably reflect your present physical reality.

I have proved for myself that through a better understanding of the mental world, it is easier to practically apply it in our lives.

Working on the Mind

By opening my mind to meditation methods and other tools that are not all about the mainstream, I ran into The Silva Method program.

You can support yourself in the next steps:

1. Invest in guidance that can help you structure your mindset. I definitely recommend *The Free Will Method* and *The Silva Method*, because those are the ones that helped me, but I am pretty sure there are so many out there, as long as it resonates with you. The idea is for you to look and find support out there because it is there.

2. Put it into practice every day.

3. Read as much as you can about the mind and surround yourself with people who actually make this seed grow and expand, that liberate and celebrate the new you.

You just need to be open.

I practiced both methods daily: I woke up, meditated; after lunch, I meditated; before sleeping, I meditated. I applied the techniques that are explained there and I still do. I am already living a different reality because I understood that reality is a vibration.

Results always come from the same principles: consistency, faith, and work. If you commit yourself to something, there is no way you cannot get that something, as long as you are doing the work.

Accessing Ancient Wisdom

Even though I was born and raised in Guatemala, I never really understood the native Mayan civilization.

In high school, we read and studied about the Mayan culture as if it belonged to the past, and Mayans no longer existed. Our approach to indigenous culture was very much from a colonized perspective, since our books were American and that created alienated perspectives from us and our own local culture. Mayan temples were simply tourist places. Mayan wisdom and cosmology were never taught.

I had to move away from Guatemala to perceive and see my country with different eyes. Later, I moved to Lake Atitlan (my current home) to get in contact with Mayans, practice with them, and learn from them. Before that, I learned about the ancient civilization of the Dradivas in India, by practicing yoga with a guru in the Himalayas, and by reading about the Indian Natives in North Americas.

Being in India for six months connected me to the roots of the Indian lands and to yoga itself. It changed my life, because I experienced yoga in a deeper way rather than just my *asana* practice, or what appears to be physical yoga.

The Importance of Thinking for Yourself

Thinking for ourselves might be one of the most important and challenging practices on a modern day-to-day basis. Politics and modern culture are weaved into and based on the economic establishment that people are said to be part of in order to to enjoy freedom and goods and rights. Really, the current world economic establishment only serves a small percentage of humanity.

People in power of economic and political resources know how to manipulate people's minds and individual's belief systems through their emotions. This knowledge goes all the way back to reptilian beings, the Annunakis, followed by Masons or Illuminati. It makes no difference whether we know or believe where it comes from. It's important to know how the system works and why, so that individuals can start awakening to their own power.

Everything that is being said and told through the media, whether or not we're conscious of it, is being whispered and programmed in our minds so that we think a certain way and act accordingly. Did you know that the food you eat, the propaganda, publicity you see is all information being implanted in your mind to avoid you being free and in control of your own personal powers?

Silent time, listening to the whispers of your heart, trusting your feelings regarding what others say and do, will lead you to your soul purpose and greatest destiny. That is why individual truth is so important because it will align us to where we need to be, what we need to do, and, essentially, to who we really are. Once an individual finds their own truth through himself, and not necessarily following a group's truth, it cannot any longer be manipulated.

Whatever is not considered truth by the media or the general public opinion, is neglected or ignored, even if information can be useful for humanity. For example, one of the first modern people who practiced healing through mind powers was Edgar Cayce (1877-1945) known as the "sleeping prophet," and the father of holistic medicine. He was one of the pioneers on channeling information or memories from a higher source to the everyday physical third dimension. People started healing through his solutions, even if modern medicine consultations would say there was no cure in the client's condition.

Hypnosis, clairvoyance, and other psychic powers are becoming more common these days, defying mainstream medicine and religion. But these could also be considered to complement modern medicine.

In the 19th century, modern and scientific medicine was just starting to thrive and whatever practice was not able to be studied or proved scientifically was considered fraud and phony, and it still does in the present moment. And, although nowadays there are more conversations around these topics and esoteric concepts, it is especially so that plant medicine and other healing and transformative practices are considered unknown or even sinful, even though these have brought constructive healing and human transformations.

Trusting Your Inner Compass

Your inner truth is connected to your inner compass.

Considering my decisions carefully has led me to choices with complete freedom regardless of other opinions, even when I felt I was foolish or an outcast. But I have grown to be courageous and to believe in myself even if it means losing people around me, because there are lots of inner and outer references that prove I am right.

What is your own authentic truth? By not accepting public opinion as global truths, we can start building a better relationship with our individuality.

Freedom is being able to choose for yourself and act upon who you are. Freedom is being who you are, enjoying who you are. A group's truth might not work for you specifically. You should follow your heart and your own truth.

Let's look for the following answers:

1. Ask how you feel about what is being sold every day on TV news or via social media. Can you see how this works for the system?

2. Consume and read other kinds of news, news that makes you feel better about yourself and about being human.

3. Once you decide not to accept a general truth — even though it is everywhere and everyone is talking about it — you can start developing your own truth. How do you feel? Go beyond what has become mere public acceptance of an idea.

If you start to connect with your own authentic self, then you won't be manipulated by the media. You will start to feel and act differently, because your openness will receive new information to your mind and body.

Polish Your Mind

Cultivating a better relationship with our human avatar and game reality, means to listen more closely to our heart: the physical link with the Source. Once we are connected to our hearts and trust its whisperings through feelings or intuitions, we will always be guided to where we need to be and what we need to do. It's like a more elevated source of information that sees it all and understands the full picture. But what does it really mean to listen to one's heart?

To make changes in our lives, we need to believe in what we feel and be courageous. This is exactly what listening to the heart means — to listen and trust your feelings, to trust this state of certainty even if all your five senses are telling you differently. It is to be connected to a wider and wiser Source in which an inner compass will direct you towards your purpose. And everything around us will tell us differently until you surround yourself with people who are already living their authentic lives.

But what happens when you feel confused? You can support yourself with the following steps:

1. Whenever in question or in doubt, look for a place of silence,

close your eyes, relax your body, find yourself in this pacific scenery in your mind, and ask your heart what feels right or wrong — the answers will always show up, and usually they are the first to pop up. This means tuning into your inner truth.

2. It takes courage to follow your heart. See yourself as a lion or a tiger — they symbolize courage and the wisdom behind the courage. Whatever path you choose, you will learn, and it will eventually lead you to the right truths, the right wisdom.

3. Take it easy. Have fun in your life. If you are confused about something, add dynamism to your life. The answer will come eventually, especially when you are not forcing yourself to find it.

Relaxing physically and mentally will always create a space within silence and truth. When you practice this every day, or every time you need to, you will start building confidence around this until you no longer question it.

Self-education and self-investment are very important, signing into courses or reading books, seminars, retreats, workshops, or any kind of investment for your inner growth. They all help to refine and redefine your knowledge about specific things, especially the ones that resonate mostly in the present time.

Continuously wanting to get better in any or every aspect of our lives is a self-love practice. Investing in yourself will get you further every time: emotionally, physically, financially, and spiritually. Live the experiences you want to have as a human being and have fun exploring what it is to be human. Be dynamic and find ways to help you change from a heavy state of consciousness to a lighter one.

What can you do to change your state of consciousness?

1. Whenever feeling low or sad or angry, go for a walk or do exercises. Do anything that will literally make you MOVE out of this space.

2. When you need clarity of mind, get yourself out of a place and move to another.

3. Fasting and changing your diet can be very helpful because it can bring more vitality and focus to your days.

I choose to believe in myself, in my superpowers, and in the certainty that I am held, guided and protected 24/7. I choose to trust being connected to my body and inner compass or intuition — I choose to believe that I am guided.

I remember clearly that I was once saved from a car crash that would have probably killed me. I was coming out of a gas station in a high speed roadway during the night, and I didn´t see a black pickup truck with no lights on coming super fast. I meant to push the accelerator on the car, because I assumed no car was coming, but I felt something or someone on my right shoulder kind of asking me to stop and not push the accelerator. Three seconds later, I saw the black pick up truck without lights passing in front of me at high speed. I cannot explain exactly what happened, but I knew that that night something prevented me from having a fatal accident.

What is your relationship with your intuition or inner compass?

1. Think about when you have been guided, either by intuition, dreams, or something a person says to you out of the blue, out of nowhere.

2. Think about when you have felt you are in the wrong place or with the wrong people. How does that make you feel, and what did you choose to do after feeling this specific way? Did you play along or decide to leave? Think about a time when you have felt something is off regarding a place, an activity, or a person.

3. Think about when you believed in yourself and decided to do something bold. What do you have complete faith in?

If you look to your past with the intention of learning from specific times and places where you have decided to trust your gut — even if it's not what everyone else is doing — you will know that it was an act of self-love even if it might seem selfish at the moment.

Once we no longer decide from a place of fear, we cease to pump the machine that the whole system relies on. We will start creating a different reality, and at the same time, experience a whole new one.

This is what hacking the reality game is all about.

The Inner Healing Process

Because we are essentially water in human form, we receive and give information all the time through and from our environment. Just as water vibrates and takes form, so, too, do we. Water is connected to our emotions, and emotions are key in the human experience. They are information that guides us and helps us understand and move in the world. But not only that, there are memories and technology held in the earthly water bodies and the crystals (solidified water) that are always transmitting information to our DNA.

Your water body needs to be open to receive this information that the bodies of water of planet Earth transmit for our evolution. The emotional body is equal to the inner child, and as as long as we are not in balance within ourselves, we won't be able to access higher frequencies because higher frequencies affect our physical bodies and our psyches. Just like trees and mycelium, water bodies have electrochemical communication between each other. It's a global network, and we can access it, upload and download memories, and essentially, upgrade our DNA if we take care of our emotional selves. That is why responsibility is key.

There is a whisper inside of us. Many people around the world have started an inner healing process and are taking their connections more seriously, because deep in ourselves, we are called to come home. As long as we are hopeful, we believe that we can create a different world.

The Book that Saved the Seas was the first novel that I wrote, based on the underwater civilization story that inspired me to do so. Through writing it, I understood that the story was coming from my heart, maybe as a memory, or maybe as hope. Something clicked inside me and I simply began to sit and write. The process of writing that book brought me clarity and opened a path for me into sharing my life with others. The story came to me in 2005 and the connection to my emotional body from the ocean itself, opened space into my healing and into receiving information from higher places that can bring answers to my readers, because it already brings answers to me. I remember during my first scuba diving dives that I didn't want to come out of the water, so I had to force myself to breathe super slowly and deeply so the tank oxygen wouldn't end. Without aiming for it, this created an inner rhythm and silence in my mind and body that entered me into a different conscious state of being. I was flying underwater, seeing it all, feeling it all — I felt both free and connected to my body at the same time. I truly believe scuba diving was the first substantial experience that gave me access to a whole new universe within and without.

It is vital to heal the inner child or emotional body, in order to access evolution. By acknowledging our emotional wounds from a compassion perspective, we can see the state of our inner child and hold it with our consciousness. Although this sounds crazy, we can time travel with our mind and hearts, so in meditation, when you hold that inner child, you, as the inner child as well, will receive the love and compassion and attention from the present self-timeline (which for your inner child is your future self).

This will automatically shift the energy in your past, present and in your future, because you are healing a very important piece of your past. Essentially, you are changing your water patterns, and therefore you can begin to receive information aligned to those new patterns. Even if your wound comes from an incredibly cruel or violent, abusive situation, part of your healing is deciding to let it go. Whatever it can be, you are no doing anyone any favor, especially yourself, by holding anger or resentment toward whoever or whatever caused it.

Sometimes we believe that we are doing ourself a favor by not letting go or forgiving. But believe me, this is only hurting you. You are still choosing to play victim — as much as this is a hard truth to digest, it is the truth.

I considered myself a victim for many years. I chose to let this go because I was tired of being conditioned by this wound of treason, not being able to trust anyone and just attracting the same pattern of people in my life, in my romantic and intimate relationships.

So how can you start to accelerate your connection with your inner powers?

- Decide to heal your inner child.

- Ask for guidance. You can always look for guidance from someone else, guiding you into an inner child meditation in which you can contact him or her and have a conversation that can start a healing.

If you connect with your inner child, he or she will let you know what is the problem or the wound, and together you will bring healing. Attention, compassion, and presence is what is required, and once you start doing this, you will probably feel lighter and lighter, freer and freer every time, no longer conditioned by your physical or emotional body, but by your higher self.

Healing the Deepest Wound

Meditation, plant medicine, and ancestral wisdom can guide and help us to understand and integrate.

Plant medicine has become very popular in the Western world, and there is a good reason for that. Plant medicine has proven to be very effective and has had long term effects on the human psyche.

Through ayahuasca I healed my deepest wound. There is always something to heal. Healing means balance. There is always something to balance. This is all part of self-knowledge and growth. The whole point of being alive is to grow and to love more through that growth.

Plants can help us remember the whole spectrum of who we really are. For example, peyote helped me heal my relationship with masculine energy, which I believe was associated with my relationship with security and money, emotions, and beliefs in my muladhara chakra, or my survival perspective on earth.

Here are other ways to approach your healing through plant medicine:

1. If you want and choose to go deeper, plant medicine will help you heal things from the core.

2. Avoid commercial plant medicine, and look for recommendations from the people who are holding the space since they have great influence in your experience. Ask the

plant before even taking it, to guide you, and it will.

3. Integrate after your experience, take some time off from your daily routine and surround yourself with people or no people, in order for you to gain clarity on your experience without being questioned.

If you feel you are ready to try plant medicine, then you probably are. You will start feeling it even before you take it.

I was deeply guided when I was 12 years old by starting to scuba dive. Maybe my actual healing started there. My family had this amazing yearly getaway every New Year when we would go scuba diving.

When I was 17, I remember waiting for the boat to come get us at the dock and go to the island, I just started imagining this whole world underwater. I decided I was going to write all of these thoughts in my notebook, and I did. I felt something in my heart — something I had never felt before — and I decided I wanted to explore what it meant. I was young and didn't know myself too well at that time, but I can still remember this calling, from the depths of the ocean, and all of these characters and stories that started to flow through my being.

I think that was the first time I thought about being a writer, and writing stories, and for the New Year's resolution that we shared at the New Year's dinner table, I said: I will write about the ocean and secrets about Jacques Cousteau. The book will be called: *The Secret Book of Jacques Cousteau*. I finally called it: *The Book that Saved the Seas*, because now I know that I intended to write a book and to heal myself through it.

Becoming Creative

Creativity is a great way to connect with your emotional body. It is a great way to channel emotions. Have you ever cried listening to music or watching a movie? Have you ever cried, felt happiness or sadness while reading a book or novel? Have you ever felt lust or power from seeing a painting?

You can actually create something from an emotion, so this emotion comes out and becomes something beautiful and deep for others, as well. Anything is possible in art. It is not about the outcome, but the process. Art is all about directing our imagination. It also helps to understand what state we are in at that particular moment, and to transform and redefine an emotion. It is about channeling our inner child at play.

Support yourself on the following steps and surrender to the process:

- Choose any kind or artistic activity or discipline that you want to follow and explore.

- Find a place and time to work on your art. Is it writing, working with clay, glass blowing, journaling or painting? Do you want to cook, sculpt, film a scene, or create music? Find the tools that you need and decide that for the next couple of hours that is all you are going to do. Don't worry about the outcome of your art, but enjoy the process.

- It is important not to judge yourself. Go crazy, go nuts. Remember it is your inner child playing.

We can feel lightness in the heart and body from creating art.

When I was 18, I felt like a rebel. I knew that if I decided to start smoking marijuana, I was going to love it. What weed represented for me at that time, represented myself. I listened to reggae music, to Bob Marley, and I was against 'the system' of society. I didn't like the capitalist and extreme right university I was in, studying business, and I decided to follow my writing and journalistic career.

At the same time, I was still in my healing process, conditioned by my physical body. I was drinking alcohol, eating poorly, hiding the truth, and, in general, I was having a hard time, and my life felt completely divided, as if I were living two different lives. This caused me stress, anger, and for me to try to avoid that with sex, alcohol, and marijuana.

Even if my whole motivation was *freedom*, I felt less free than I had ever felt before. I can see now that I was avoiding feelings and my reality. I was deeply rooted in fear and guilt. I also know that, free from addictions on drugs, I can be free from addictive relationships. This helped me heal my water body or physical body, and therefore, brought to me my connection with my inner child, which eventually brought healing and real freedom from triggering emotions.

Addictions usually are brought as coping mechanisms to avoid feeling and hurting, and they are often associated with trauma, beliefs, emotions and, above all, our perspective and stories we tell ourselves. If you understand the stories behind certain actions or addictions, and change them, you might as well free yourself from whatever is holding you down.

Being responsible in healing our physical bodies is also being open to receive new and higher information that will take us to our next evolutionary step, which is the one of being conscious of the reality game and playing it from our higher self.

CHAPTER 3

Science and the Dimension of Magic

Until an experience is lived and integrated in our being, felt and transformed into knowledge, it will always be something abstract, conceptual, and external. When something has been experienced, it can be used as a tool and powerful information. It becomes practical, involving the actual doing and being, rather than with just theories and ideas.

As I have mentioned, the idea of magic as something that we witness instead of experiencing, has alienated humans into alchemizing reality. Turning the chemistry of something to something different is a daily natural human act, so it all comes down to believing and knowing how we are doing it consciously, so we can direct it better. A single thought or emotion changes the chemistry of your brain and body and, therefore, your whole reality. The way you breathe influences your nervous system, which in turn affects the chemistry of how information is processed, delivered, and interpreted. It directly affects your decision-making, which again changes your reality.

Can magic really be applied as a science? Is it something that can be applied now by the inexperienced in an intentional and systematic manner? The answer is yes.

Electricity works in our bodies as it does elsewhere. It provides energy for the body to function.

Light and energy are essentially the same thing. Our bodies are conductors of this energy or light simply by existing and being alive. When we direct this energy consciously, acting upon our decisions, we start to understand through experience and practice how to conduct and create with this energy.

What pulse keeps the heart beating and signals our brains to do this and that? The body, connected to the source of energy that keeps it alive, will eventually die, but the energy that keeps the body alive will be transformed into something else.

Acknowledging this energy or light that keeps our body alive is how we start to understand and make use of this source of energy.

The Law of Attraction — the process of manifesting a reality by believing and creating a feeling inside that resonates to that reality — implies that even if we are not aware of it, we are creating our reality all the time. Consciousness never ceases to be, so even when you are sleeping, you are emitting a frequency that will eventually transform into a physical reality. Consciously or unconsciously, we are always directing our energy. The difference is that once we consciously press the button, that light or energy will follow our will.

This energy is originally and essentially directed by our thoughts. It's necessary to be aware of our thoughts, otherwise we're simply using our energy to react to the outer world.

Understanding the science behind the creative process might help you to find better ways of using it and become more confident in your own creative process.

Our different experiences might be considered to be coincidences until we become conscious that we produce them through our mindset and belief system. We conduct our energy and light within us, within our own channeling system, and the universe responds to our inner reality with an outer reality. It is, in its highest potential, being able to create thoughts that generate a faster vibration than the speed of light that fully taps into the quantum field where eventually, we can literally create matter out of a thought.

It is all about aligning our chakras in coherence fractal patterns, enlightening our energy field of electric buzzing fire and then reversing our energy field inward.

Creating a New Reality

Thoughts are energy. They can be as big and as solid as a conviction: a belief or idea that we will defend as true, even if it costs us our lives. Conviction is the deepest form of belief.

By knowing that you have power inside, your own source of light that you can choose to direct through your body and through the physical world, by being it, will reveal a hidden and unknown universe for you and, eventually for the world. Because the source of light and inner magical powers have always been there and are responding to you. All the time, as long as your heart is beating.

Whatever you are living today in the physical realm — your body, your house, your work, your partnership, your financial status — is a product of your past decisions and your past self-consciousness. It is a reflection of your past choices and thoughts. It is not really your present self-consciousness, because your free will is getting you to change your perspective on this present physical reality, or in other words, your creation of your past self. So now that you have a different perspective, you can start to change your thoughts, therefore your emotions and actions, and create a different future and present based on a different consciousness state. You will experience then, in a near future, the reflection of your present inner state.

Electric Living by Kolie Crutcher, a book written by an electrical engineer, explains scientifically how the creation process works, starting from the thought, to an emotion, and on to the materialization of a feeling into reality. And it confirmed to me that the physical reality is all energy and is always vibrating, responding to the observer, to you. If we really understand this, then I think that we would start creating a system of methods and conduct actions to create the results that we are looking for.

Many books, documentaries, and movies talk about related topics and concepts, such as *The Power of Now* by Eckhart Tolle, and most of the work of Joe Dispenza. Once we start to understand our own relationship with these amazing aspects of who we are, the power of our thoughts, understanding that everything is energy and that we are the source and directors of this energy, life can become deeply exciting, joyful, and free.

The more I practice, the more I know that I am the creator of my physical reality.

Magic Is the Science of Sciences

Magic is the science of sciences, because it is linked to the Source of it all. It is a conductor of the ultimate Source toward the vision in the mind. Although the ultimate Source itself cannot be studied, there are patterns around it that can help us have a more rational approach to it. The consciousness or the eyes that see the light, has influence on the light — the light starts bringing particles together based on what the observer is projecting or focusing on. Essentially, it is then, where we focus our attention, the energy that we are connecting to and materializing. By your choices, you are the conductor of the light.

I believe and know that we all crave for real freedom, and that freedom comes from creating from deeper states of being. Being free starts from the idea of being free to choose differently, which comes from being free to think differently. So how can you understand and explore these concepts for yourself?

1. Read *Electric Living*, written by Kolie Crutcher, to understand, through the eyes of an electrical engineer, from a scientific point of view, the process behind creating out of, what it seems, nowhere.

2. Prove it for yourself. What you are living today in the physical matter is the creation of your past self.

3. Start to write and repeat mantras regarding your new self. Where is your focus? What are your beliefs? What emotions are you harboring? Repeat as soon as you wake up: *I am a creator. I am creating a beautiful life. What am I feeling right now? The feeling is the answer to the following question: What am I creating right now?*

Practice brings mastery. It might seem to be difficult at the beginning, but through practice, you become a new self and naturalized. You have created a new state of being, you can do this all the times you want through the polishing of yourself in your journey.

The first time I put my creative powers into practice, I was in Indonesia about to fly to India. I didn't know where I was going or how long, all I wanted was to be guided, and I decided I was. My intention was creating a journey that would guide me through synchronicities.

Everyone asked me what my plans were, where I would sleep, how long I would be traveling, if I had life insurance, etc. and I didn't have any of those answers. People who cared for me were worried and seriously asked for me to be responsible because India was a dangerous country for solo travelers like me. But I knew that I didn't want my journey to be guided by fear, precautions, and definite planning. I knew that I would know where and when to go and how, day by day.

The day before leaving Indonesia, I met Étienne, a French musician who gave me my first clue. He had just come from India, and he deeply suggested I should go to Leh, in the Himalayas. He showed me some pictures, and I knew that was my first signal. I was open to synchronicities, and synchronicities appeared for me, guiding me to amazing people and amazing experiences that I take deeply in my heart. In Leh, I met two of my really good current friends, from Israel, who again guided me to another town, in which I met other people who guided me to other places.

I was an open book. I was shaved, I didn't have a name, I was willing to work with my darkness and my pain, I was willing to sit by and with myself and go in. And even though my journey in India was hard sometimes, because I felt deep void and loneliness, I also got what I was looking for: myself. I had the most amazing gift of studying with a Naga guru, who shared with me his wisdom and agreed to make me his disciple, which is very rare nowadays. I realized, by being open and innocent, I was also attracting tools for my greater self: through people, books, conversations and mostly: feelings. I wrote my second novel based on this journey, called *The Game of Crystals*.

Once you realize how you can tap and use these powers, you can start playing with them and dive deeper.

How can you start focusing your powers?

1. Once you have tapped into your powers, it is very important to solidify it and build your certainty around it.

2. If you do one thing once and then you stop practicing or building around it, it can dissipate and go away.

3. Put into practice your powers daily, by constantly creating new things in your life. Not from a place or state from lacking or not enough, but from a place of wonder and gratefulness. Remember you don't need to do anything really, but you deserve to have amazing human experiences. So instead of creating from a place of need or look, create from a place of being deserving.

4. Change your words around it: Instead of saying, I need to have this or to feel this, say: I deserve to experience this or experience feeling this. Become.

5. If you put your powers into practice, you will become a master in your own process and will solidify certainty, faith, and magic around your life.

> *"No, I would not want to live in a world without dragons,*
> *as I would not want to live in a world without magic,*
> *for that is a world without mystery,*
> *and that is a world without faith."*
>
> — *R.A. Salvatore*

The Heart Is the Creator of the Mind

Through my process, I discovered my truth of being a creator, which is the one of being in the heart.

There are no more creative beings than children. They seem to live in a different dimension where time and seriousness don't exist. There is no past, there is no future, there is just what they are experiencing. This state, the state of heart consciousness, the place where we belong is a different dimension, because the heart is a portal by itself. It is the dimension of magic, because it is where we remember and experience our limitlessness, therefore we use and experience limitless form. That is why when from the heart, we are most creative, because creativity comes from the limitless. How can we create if we perceive things as limited? Isn't imagination the fuel for your dreams?

Being in the heart, as children, in awe, is also expecting the best and feeling things as they come and go without fear or judgment. How do we get disconnected from that? How do we transition from being born in innocence into an ego or fear based consciousness? The creators of mainstream truths want you to feel far from home, because if you no longer need anything, in a consumption behavioral state, then the established system will cease to exist. So as soon as they can take you out of home and make you forget about it, the better it is for them.

You will learn at a young age that being in the heart is unsafe because, as long as people don't know or trust themselves, naturally they will distrust. You become protective of your feelings and of your innocence.

Throughout history people — especially men — have closed their hearts because of their upbringing. Nowadays, even if we are not particularly in a real survival situation, we have to learn how to be in our hearts and feel safe in our bodies. Being in the heart or having an open heart is — according to public opinion reflected in movies, news, and social dynamics — lame and weak, because when you are weak you are vulnerable, and being vulnerable is dangerous.

The science behind the creative process is deeply connected to the heart. So as long as your heart is closed or you are not connected to it, it will be particularly hard to be a true creator. The heart is the creator of the mind.

Liberate Yourself through Your Heart

"My technique is, don't believe anything
— if you believe in something, you are
automatically precluded from believing its opposite."

— Terence McKenna (1946-2000), ethnobotanist and mystic

The only thing we should worry about believing is in ourselves. It is the only belief that won't separate us from others, because believing that we are capable of creating what we choose to create will allow us to live the life we deserve.

When you follow your heart, even if you are rejected from a group, you will be guided to people who will liberate and celebrate your own unique being instead of rejecting it and make you feel bad or wrong about yourself and taking away your innocence.

So, how to access the heart-consciousness state? To connect with the heart we need first to make the choice of healing it.

This might mean letting go of resentment, anger, guilt, and unforgiveness to ourselves and to others, and taking care of our heart when we are sad. When feeling sad, honoring the sadness, listen to it and release it. Emotions are nothing more than information that is passing through you and is telling you something about yourself. So simply listening, instead of avoiding, will let any emotion find its way out. Being responsible for our hearts is vital to feel safe and connected to this portal that lives within us.

When hearts open, we become open to love and being loved. A sense of innocence, wonder, joy and effortlessness are some of the qualities of being in this state — it is for me, then, the dimension of magic: to be open and expect the best, being in the present, a witness of life, a true creator, from a place of joy and union.

Our heart is a portal. The space in our heart is timeless and spaceless because it is space and time itself. You can experience this place by closing your eyes and going back to any memory of your past and experiencing emotions and feelings around that memory.

You are now creating your future by how you are thinking and feeling. The different and infinite spectrum of possible futures that await you are being chosen by you, consciously or unconsciously, by your connecting to specific frequencies in your heart. You can tune into whatever future you deserve by feeling like you already are experiencing, from a place of gratitude and not from lack or need. And by tuning your heart to that specific frequency, you are vibrating in that frequency, the one that aligns with that future.

You can also close your eyes and choose to see the beautiful things in your present moment: people whom you love, like your family and friends. You can acknowledge and feel gratitude about waking up and going to sleep in a warm and cozy bed, eating delicious food, having a brain and eyes that can actually read and help you bring new information into your mind, etc. You can also wake up in the morning and simply be happy that you are alive and have faith that the mystery of it will bring you amazing experiences and fun adventures. If you are present, you are conscious of what thoughts are in your mind and what you are creating.

See With Your Heart

It's easy to lose your way when you see with your eyes and not with your heart. That's because frequencies on the outside will pull you out. This is why meditation is so important, because one returns to one's center and can connect with the frequency of abundance and wealth. In other words, one connects with the inner creator. You are certain that you are the creator and, therefore, you are in the dimension of magic.

Synchronizing with the heart is closing the senses, returning to the soul and seeing, feeling, listening, smelling, and basically vibrating with your amazing dream future from there. It is key to know and be certain that we are already that person who has everything that you have dreamt of.

The challenge is to block the apparent physical reality and tune to your heart frequency, until eventually you no longer need to block anything.

There are going to be moments when we feel sad or angry or anything that is not necessarily happiness. But being in peace and acceptance with that, as well, is something incredible and powerful. It is not about avoiding it — it is about feeling, but also letting go, whenever you know it's already too much of being sad, and you decide, 'Okay, I am done feeling sad. I might feel sad again about this, but today I will choose to go out with a friend or take a longer walk or write about it.' Feelings and emotions need to be honored, listened to, and then they go away. But mostly, something that might have happened to you 2 weeks ago, 5 months ago, 3 years ago, or 5 or even 15 years ago, might be something that you are still carrying inside.

And, therefore, it is probably a burden and attachment to either an identity, a story, or the role of playing victim.

You can do the following exercises:

1. Meditate or simply be aware of how you are feeling. Do you feel something in your heart space?

2. Do you feel resentment towards you or someone else? Are you judging yourself for something you did or happened to you? How do you see yourself? What is the story behind your wounds and yourself?

3. Practice compassion. Can you add compassion around this feeling or emotion? Can you love the things that you don't like or even detest about yourself? Can you love your wound? Can you love your offender? See how your heart starts becoming warmer and warmer by just stopping to judge yourself or others, and simply be accepting and loving, even if it seems impossible.

4. Remember that you deserve to feel free, so it is not about someone else, it is about you. Keep that in mind so you can always come back to yourself, the most important person in your life.

Adding compassion to your heart will open it. Every time you feel harsh inside, compassion will start warming and releasing harshness around your heart and your inner child. You will slowly start creating a relationship between you and the dimension of magic, your home. We have all been there; we just need to re-learn how to stay there and create a sustainable life that can sustain ourselves and our worlds there, inviting others to create them for themselves.

Practicing Unconditional Love

What does unconditional love mean? I would say it means being able to love yourself and your family as they are, without wanting them to be different. It is difficult, though, to love them as they are. As humans, we have a lot of expectations, based on ourselves, about our beliefs of happiness, success and worth.

Here are some exercises for you:

1. Practice unconditional love on yourself. Can you accept who you are? Can you accept your choices, such as habits that you know you shouldn't have?

2. Can you think about why you think or believe you should be different than you are? Can you hear these voices, maybe from your parents or teachers, that have lacked self-compassion and therefore projected this on you some time ago (or even in the present)? How does this make you feel? Do you feel tense, or wrong, or bad?

3. Can you choose to love yourself, and absolutely everything that has brought you to this specific time and moment? Remember that what you are living now, is your creation. And as long as we don´t love or accept our present creation, that comes from an old self, we cannot set it free.

Loving and accepting something makes it free. If you apply this perspective and attitude to yourself, you will start seeing the world through different lenses, and people will start blooming around you, because they feel safe and accepted by you. You are not only giving yourself and them the gift of just being, you are letting yourself and others to make mistakes and open up to life.

How Our Words Recall Our Creation

Words bring energy from within. Words control the inner flow and fire with specific vibration through sounds with meanings. There is a huge difference between saying nice to meet you to someone just out of courtesy, from saying nice to meet you to someone we're really interested in. Our whole body is vibrating differently when we really feel what we are saying, and, therefore, we are creating an energy wave that most probably the person that is receiving this word can feel and respond positively to.

"Words and magic were in the beginning one and the same thing."

— *Sigmund Freud*

Our bodies have two specific energy vortexes or chakras that create. The first one is found in the *genital area* or *sacrum*, and the second one in our throat or voice. Here we're exploring the one in your throat, which emerges in the form of voice or sound vibrations.

Many people, through misunderstanding themselves, have dissonance or unbalance in their throat, or because they are saying something not true to them, even if they don´t know it, or they are consciously telling lies or feel afraid to speak out.

This center will then start to get blocked with information of fear, which will reflect this dissonance and will ask to be addressed and balanced. Since a lot of us have been silenced and abused in the past or present, as growing up culturally or personally, being told repeatedly that our voice or opinion is not important or we should remain silent, we can start expressing unbalanced behaviors such as speaking too much, or too fast, not knowing when to stop, not making sense in our word choice, or the opposite: feeling that our voice is not important and undeserved to be heard so we don´t say anything at all, even if the right conditions are inviting us to do so.

The power behind our words and prayers is deeply connected to our creative powers. That is why every civilization in the past and in the present moment, practices systematic repetition of affirmations, prayers, mantras, and chants since it is a way to become, because what is being said and expressed has an effect on life. We create from our words and specifically, from the feeling and strength behind these words. Most successful people practice affirmations and a lot of them even write them on paper so as to ground these words into the physical world.

Each time you say thank you to the things that come into your life, and feel the gratitude behind them, you are creating abundance in your life. You are appreciating the richness around you and by saying so, you are acting upon it, solidifying the gratitude state inside. Therefore, you create more abundance in your life. The opposite also happens — if you are constantly complaining, you are creating more things to complain for.

Once you know that what you say, and how you say it, is creating something all the time, start applying it, through the repetition of mantras, affirmations, and thanking absolutely everything that is, that goes and that comes. Spells, or magic spells, come from spelling specific words in specific ways. The magic spell is a *verbal formula believed to have magic force*, and, yes, this magic force comes from within, from your own passion and belief around the spell. And it is expressing God. From a universal law point of view: the vibration turned into words that comes out of you is creating. That's why what you say, and how you say it, is creating something. The Bible also says, *in the beginning was the Word, and the Word was with God, and the Word was God. All things were made through him, and without him was not anything made that was made.*

Since you have always been the creator of everything in your life, let's analyze the following:

1. Think about specific times in your life in which you have said something so deeply from your gut that it has felt so powerful.

2. What is it that you deserve? What is it that you are creating? Now that you already know, think and write about mantras or affirmations that are aligned to these. It could be like: *I am grateful for my health. I am grateful for my spectacular partner and relationship. I am grateful for this amazing meal that is making me beautiful and healthy. I am grateful for this glass of water that is cleansing my body and bringing light into my body.*

3. Somewhere, write down these affirmations and mantras so you can see them daily.

Fear of Expressing Yourself Holds You Back

Sometimes holding back can cause us harm. Secrets, fear of not saying something to someone, or not validating yourself enough to express your needs, have a negative effect on your body. Energy will start piling up in your throat, which can lead to unbalance there, affecting your voice.

Your voice is a portal of who you are. What you say is a reflection of your current state of being.

Here are some steps on how to start practicing the creative use of your voice:

1. Be careful with your words. Only speak when you have to;

appreciate silence and listen actively to others.

2. Practice silence. Silence is also a way of saying something.

3. The more careful you are with your words, the more you'll learn how to use your voice effectively.

4. Observe and listen to your inner dialogue, as well. How do you talk to yourself in your own intimacy? What do you say every time you look in the mirror or take a shower? What do you say to yourself?

Are you ready to use your voice to create abundance?

The Conscious and Unconscious Mind

The person who is completely attached to the body through the five senses, and who has forgotten that he or she is more than a body, believes that what has been experienced in the third dimension or physical reality, is all that is. This is what I call getting lost in the reality game.

With such a limited sense of self, a person experiences life in a limited way. The mind of the individual is only connected to and reacting to the information that comes from these five senses.

But what if the spark that keeps the body alive is an expression of the Source of all — God? Then we would know that we were having a human experience. We are humans, but also limitless beings, an individual expression of the creator of all. We are limitless souls inside a human body, experiencing and growing through the physical reality, learning about the pleasures of the body and to practice unconditional love and certainty, since it is challenging here. The real challenge is that as incarnated souls, we tend to forget who we are because part of the exploration is to discover and remember who we are.

Through meditation, we can start reconceptualizing the concepts that we have learned and used to construct a false self. Meditation is a tool to practice self-observation and being present, connecting to our inner truth and to our higher self. It is to experience a greater sense of being that transcends the idea of being just a body.

I call it meditation practice, because it is through practice that one becomes a master of oneself.

My daily practice of yoga, breathwork, and meditation created the right atmosphere for me to see what was conditioning me.

Since a young age, I have experienced out-of-body experiences and lucid dreaming. Even though I was not able to put these experiences into words, I had a sense of being able to transcend my body. And by experiencing the plant medicine ayahuasca, I really navigated through The Mind.

I understood, then, that my mind, connected to my five senses in the body, was an extension of The Mind, and even if my mind depended on me and my super limited awareness, The Mind was everything that is, the ocean of life itself, and my mind simply a drop. The Mind is the Universal Mind. It is the orchestrator of everything that is. It is God. It is the Source. And in its Mind, in its thoughts, in this dream and game, we live and explore. We are a creation of this big creation, The Mind. But we also do have an individual mind, our mind, which is also known as consciousness. Our mind is our consciousness, our focus. Where is your mind at now? Reading these words, right? And since The Mind is already everything that is and is not, the only way for The Mind to know our mind and to express itself in our world (mind in this specific time and space) is through our awareness, where we choose to place our focus and what we are seeing.

This experience played a huge part in my healing and awakening.

The Wisdom That Comes from Experience

As the Incas say, "The real gold is not gold itself, but the wisdom that comes out of experiences." There is no more valuable thing than this kind of gold, and the conquistadors didn't understand it.

Through meditation, I started to know myself.

To bring more understanding into your meditations, you can ask yourself the following:

1) Think about yourself. The Mind already contains every possibility that you choose to focus on. The poor version of you. The rich version of you. The healthy version of you. The successful version of you. The victim version of you. Now that you get it, what of all possible versions are you choosing to live or experience? Which one are you feeling (choosing)?

2) What would it **feel** to be that higher version of yourself? If it's the healthy, abundant, successful one? Remember your present moment is a creation of your past, therefore, you are creating the future self in this present moment. Just choose which one you deserve and practice tuning to the equal vibration 24/7.

Feel it, create it. You can do this, this is your power, because the mind is The Mind itself expressing through solidified consciousness, or YOU, your Oness.

> *"We do not need magic to transform our world.*
> *We carry all of the power we need inside ourselves already."*
>
> *– J.K Rowling*

Exploring the Shadows

The darkness represents the shadow, the unknown, or what we have not yet seen, but it is part of what is. It conditions our mind and our decision making.

Meditation allows us to see what unconscious beliefs — our shadow — condition our present through the repetition of actions, patterns, and bringing light into this shadow.

Apply the image of ocean and darkness to your own self. The shadow is not your enemy or something to be scared of. It is simply something that you have not yet seen.

There is always going to be something that we are not seeing, since seeing it all, completely, is larger than ourselves. If we are starting our healing practice, it is important to ask some questions regarding what triggers us constantly, to see the repetitive patterns in our lives like, for example, the prototypes of partners that we constantly attract, or experiences that keep on repeating in our lives.

Healing is not supposed to be serious or hard.

Let's look for possible patterns:

1. Be honest with yourself.

2. Journal or make a list of patterns regarding your most intimate relationships. Are there qualities that are repetitive in your partners? A certain kind of personality or dynamic? Have there been struggles or hurts? What are your biggest fears of insecurities around a partnership?

3. Practice feeling secure without the need to have a partner, job, or payroll to make you feel secure. We really don't need anything to feel secure. This can help you choose from a better place, and discern if there are any codependent behaviors.

4. Think about your working environment. Are there qualities that are repetitive in your jobs? A certain kind of dynamic? What kind of roles have you played in your work area? How did they end (if they have)? Has there been any kind of struggle or hurting involved? Have they started a certain way and ended up a different way? What are your beliefs regarding your job or work?

The key is understanding how the Universal mind or The Mind, and your mind, come together. The Mind is the observer and the creator of it all, known as God and the Source, and "the mind" is a micro-representation of it and it is through our individuality that The Mind is exploring itself.

As long as we do not limit or condition ourselves into being the mind only — our egos and individuals selves — we are free to navigate and to open ourselves from the consciousness and the movement of The Mind, living an everflowing connection with The Source, from a physical individual form.

CHAPTER 4

Magic, the Most Practical Tool

Deep inside, you already know who you are, but, most importantly, who you are not.

By identifying or attaching ourselves to our stories, to a personality, a character that we have been playing for a while, is letting other people or circumstances tell our story. Doing this is feeling a certain way based on your expectation of what the results of acting this way will provide.

You are the consciousness inside a female, male, or ungendered, fluid body. You are the observer (conscious mind) behind the explorer of this game reality that is connected to an avatar or persona. You choose and decide how to experience the game reality.

The conscious process of creation will change you, because it requires you to connect, discover and create from different layers of who you are, rather than being attached to a character that limits you.

Being authentic and raw are qualities of being connected to your inner truth. If you no longer identify or are attached to your character, you stop taking things personally, because you now see that whatever other people do or say, is simply a reflection of their own perspective.

You are already the person you long to be. If you decide you are complete already, a brute diamond that is finding its way, an active creator of an amazing life, then life will start shifting into realizing and acknowledging all of the potential that exists in you already. Your focus turns into becoming that diamond, allowing your inner light to shine, instead of looking for the shining outside. You can actually take a pause and enjoy what you are and what you already have.

As Michalangelo said about the process of creating one of his most iconic works, the statue of David: "The sculpture is already complete within the marble block, before I start my work. It is already there, I just have to chisel away the superfluous material."

By building a better you, just as Michelangelo with David, the *you* already within you will start coming to life.

Recovering Your Power

Empowerment comes from recovering your power. This could be applied to a relationship, to a system, to an institution, to a person, to an addiction — to anything, really.

Empowerment is breaking free and bringing parts of yourself that once were scattered and given to outside elements, to outer circumstances that are always changing, and that are out of your control. You literally can feel the difference when you call the things back to your own self.

What you wish to receive from the outside, you can give yourself:

1. Ask yourself and journal, where or with whom could your power be dissipated? Is it an addiction, a person, a job, or a system?

2. Ask and journal, what would I do if I had all the power and all the energy and vitality to create something? If something is stopping you, ask yourself what belief is stopping you?

3. Remember that the opinion about yourself is more important than the opinions others have about yourself.

4. Remember we are growing and outgrowing our past self all the

time. If you had all the power, then why not dream 1000 or 100,000 times higher and bigger? Try it out.

Recognizing yourself and who you are is the most important thing you can do for yourself.

Recognize yourself:

1. Ask yourself and journal about: Do you do certain things to receive compliments or approval from others? It could be your parents, friends, partners, or society. Are you mostly motivated from outer recognition, rather than inner recognition?

2. Stop over-pleasing people and putting somebody else's opinion before yours. Stop looking for recognition outside, but recognize yourself first.

3. Can you act regardless of what others say or think? Do you understand that you are enslaved by approvals from others?

4. Think about what you would do if no one would see your deeds. Would you still be doing what you are doing?

These sorts of questions will help free you from other people's expectations and live a life that is more true to you. Simply be who you are, without fear of showing yourself. It might look like selfishness for others, but it is self-love and self-esteem, and it is important to trust your truth in this.

You Are the Sun

We human beings feed from sunlight that is transformed into different things on the ground: plants, animals, and water.

Without sunlight, there would be absolutely nothing alive on the planet. Everything lives as a perfect symbiosis in the ecosystem that feeds and contributes to each other's living being in its own way.

Here are some steps to create a better relationship with your body:

1. Recognize what the body needs to survive, such as food, sleep, warmth.

2. Drink plenty of water, reduce the amount of alcohol, stop adding processed food into your body.

3. You can start fasting for 14 hours, slowly growing into 19 hours. Consulting with a professional about this will help you understand, according to your goals and physiology and health, what kind of fasting and diet can help you the most. Fasting resets our body and helps us release toxins and restore our organs.

Here are some other ways to become more connected and sensitive to your body and understand your energy levels.

1. A regular practice of yoga or other practice can help you connect your mind and body so you can learn from yourself and how to control your breath and energy levels. Physical movement releases stuck emotions from the body and helps you get out of the mind and into the body, which will make you feel safer and clearer in the body.

2. You might practice celibacy for a period. This will give you a better idea of your energy value and value it as a sacred currency.

3. Choose who you are sleeping with more thoughtfully, and feel the energy that the other person is giving you before you deepen the link through sexual activities.

4. Walk barefoot everyday, at least for 10 to 15 minutes. Spending time in nature, removing weed from grass, or being in contact with trees or mud, help to neutralize the nervous system and nurture it by receiving energy from the Earth.

5. Sleep eight hours a day.

The power of the mind can heal basically many things in the body. Here are some examples on how you can start using your mind and magic to change your physical body:

1. Read *The Habit of Losing Yourself* and other books written by Joe Dispenza.

2. Put in practice your mind powers and shifting your physicality through *The Silva Method* or *The Free Will Method*.

3. Plant medicines can help cure the source of physical symptoms, by balancing the emotional source of the disease or by unbalancing the emotional source.

4. Change your beliefs and expectations that condition your physical functioning based on having a certain age.

Meditation is the best tool you can start using now, because it will make you realize where you are focusing and what it is that you are always building with your mind.

CHAPTER 5

The Stories They Tell Us

Everything happening in the world comes from decisions made in the past that lead us to decide differently in the present moment.

The behavior in these shifting cycles of humanity dictate and represent humanity's state of mind in a specific moment. Right now, the collective reality we are experiencing is an ego-centered consciousness, exploring our own relationship with power. It is part of our human experience to grow and to get to the next state of consciousness, our own relationship with our hearts. This ego-centered consciousness (which has played with power through wars, polarity, separation, and fear) is also an understanding of our individuality, personal power, and our human capacities, in which potentiality can be directed through awareness into creating incredible things and solutions — things that eventually will stop looking to control or to separate, but to collaborate, bringing us a better life and unlimited creativity, away from a purely survival mindset.

We are entering a time where this huge change is finally coming into physical existence in a more obvious way. This fear-based consciousness state is becoming more obvious as well. There is a resistance from those holding power, who fight to keep it.

It comes down to choosing love or fear in the most subtle layers:

thoughts, and acting upon this choice, by creating more of the same or more of the new, either protecting the old or creating the new. And paradoxically, acting through love, even in fear.

We are creating our future by how we are thinking, acting and feeling now.

This fine line that we are crossing collectively brings an amazing opportunity for souls and humans to create a different present and future for humanity. If you are reading these words and they resonate with you, there is a huge chance that you are already one of these people, since you already understand and feel that the story being told doesn't resonate with you. You have awakened and begun to understand the narrative behind the system that is deeply rooted into the human collective psyche that wants everyone to believe that there is no choice and there is no true power.

That is why magic and empowerment— your inner powers, believing in yourself and in your heart — are key to the transition humanity is experiencing. Simply by being present in love here and now is enough. We sometimes think we need to be doing big things, and feel pressure to become someone important, but just by being here in your body, open and relaxed, you are anchoring the energy that is an essential part of humanity's new reality. Simply by being aware of the following questions, you are already choosing the future:

- What are you feeling now?

- Are you anchoring love through your body to the third dimension, to the physical reality?

- Can you see it is as simple as that? You are creating the future now. That is your power.

We're already creating a different reality by giving life to different systems that are not feeding the main one. Once we start questioning everything, we start finding our own true answers.

Life as a Game Reality

Once we stop accepting and listening to the story that is being fed to us, we start to create our own personal story. This has been my favorite part of being alive, not only because naturally I am drawn into storytelling and exploring the depth of the experiences that I experience, but also because the more obvious the illusion of separation is, the more creative I can be, and the most creative I can be is by creating my own life, from the inside to the outside. I decided to perceive life as a game reality, because joy, play, love, and freedom are one of my foundations of life.

I am the observer behind the exploration of my game reality, such as when I played my favorite video games with my brothers and sister when I was younger.

As the explorer of this metaverse that I like to call a game reality, I chose a female human body or ego named Cindy. Cindy is the explorer of the physical reality connected to the game reality and receives constant information through five senses that I, the observer, perceive and decide how to process. Besides those five very obvious senses that produce different sensations in my body, there are also other senses such as the intuition or sixth sense which is the most powerful one, and from which I experience a multidimensionality, guidance, and from where I keep the connection of who I really am inside the body.

Just as in dreams where we experience real emotions, adventures, and nightmares, the same happens in this game reality. It is the moment that we forget that we are playing and exploring this reality, that we might become frustrated, serious, harsh, and disconnected from our hearts. Movies like *Avatar*, *Matrix* or *Ready Player One* are perfect examples of what I am expressing, but also video games and, lately, mostly technology is showing how a virtual reality experience creates the same brain connections and the ability to create emotions, a deep and life changing experience, such as the physical reality.

When awakening and realizing that the physical reality is just a dream and a game reality, a mind creation, we lose the fear of death because the sense of separation disappears. We no longer believe that we die along with our bodies, shifting greatly our sense of self, because radically, we start to experience the experiences differently. We start to see from a broader perspective and experience a deeper sense of who we are, regardless of the body.

We become the alchemists we already are, able to transform any experience, even the tragedies, into gold. The reality of the physical dimension is like a virtual reality where we all play the game of life.

By incarnating in these beautiful bodies, our souls tend to forget who we are. Our consciousness (the observer) is only exploring what the physical senses are perceiving. We believe that what we see, hear, smell, taste, and touch, is all that is.

Designing your Avatar

Through meditation, reading and experiencing different altered states of consciousness, I have remembered and nurtured who I am. I am already my higher self and part of my commitment is to sustain these high-vibration frequencies in my body so that my higher energy can anchor more and more to the physicality. It is essential to keep myself balanced and centered, to be present and attuned in my freedom, power, fun — and the certainty of who I am and the game that I am playing.

Warning! Changing our narrative on our life's story could have very powerful effects in our lives.

Let's play for a moment. Let's pretend you are a soul, a drop of the ocean that chose to come to Earth as a human ego and you are about to incarnate inside a body that will have a specific name, family, abilities in a specific place and time. Part of the game plan is that when you incarnate in a human body, you will forget your soul's purpose and you will forget you are a soul that actually chose this experience. Part of the game is to walk through the darkness so we can remember our light. Are you ready? Okay!

Welcome to Earth! Your name is XXX you were born in YYY in a particular body, in ZZZ country under this economic and social status, cultural values, including religion and work ethics, etc.

The challenge is that everything in this game reality will tell you what you should like and how you should spend the time here, before you can even stop and think about how you feel. It will tell you what is good and right to do or not to do, before you can even think about what feels good and wrong.

But then you remembered for a moment that it was all a game! Now you have chosen to stop identifying with your body avatar and personality, you now know that the body avatar and personality is called Ego and it has a very important purpose in life, which is that of your survival, growth, and thriving in the game. It is your main opponent and friend, a tool that if used correctly will bring you everything that you need and design — it is actually amazing!

The Ego will ask you to feed it with food because the body needs food to survive. It will ask you to acknowledge your qualities. It will ask you to exercise and feel good in your body, to say no to certain situations and to look for physical pleasure such as sex, good food, and comfort.

But if you are not on top of your Ego, it can start making you believe that you are better or less than other avatars, because it can start making you compare and compete with others to feel good by depending on external approval. It can make you believe that you should protect yourself from the world because everyone wants to get you. Essentially, it will show you how to grow and learn from love, because being alive in a human avatar is Ego, and it's meant to achieve evolution.

If you are unaware of this powerful tool and its programming— it will start to guide you. As a result, your soul can start to grow cold. Because the whole game reality is made out and sustained of a specific energy called love, the game is going to challenge you to create, grow, and to experience love. The whole point of playing is to experience love, to receive and give love. Self-love comes from the Ego, because, if you think you are not deserving of love, then you are not learning how to receive it, which leads to not learning how to give it.

Playing the Reality Game

Now you can see what kind of resources and other tools and talents you have. It could be anything that you can offer to the world as an exchange currency and, therefore, by being useful to the world, you will receive a currency called *money*. The game and your opponents will make you stronger, wiser, and sharpen your tools.

There is no point in playing a game without opponents, right?

Unless you know who you are, and that it is all a game reality, you will be controlled by the game itself.

Here is how to play the reality game:

1. See yourself as a player inside a video game. What is your avatar like? What are the resources, tools, and talents of your avatar?

2. Make a list of 3 things of each one of the following questions:

   a. What kind of human experiences would you want to experience?

   b. What growth is required for you to live this experience?

   c. What contribution or impact are you giving back to the world through these experiences?

3. Ask the following questions: Now that you know who you are behind the avatar, and you know that what is sustaining and is the Source of the the game is a specific kind of energy called love, regardless of what other avatars and other players are doing, then, if you would continuously choose love and have certainty of love and what you are creating comes from love, wouldn't you be working with the Source of it all? Wouldn't you be an extension of the Creator itself if you are connected to it? Wouldn't you be able to create from the same energy in which all is created? Wouldn't you be able to do and become magic, changing the physical reality since you are connected to the main Source of power?

If you remember who you are and are able to decide from that, you are tapping into your highest self, bringing heaven to earth. Our soul, an extension of love and God itself, represents our inner potential.

Remembering your higher self is the potentiality of your being. It is you already, believing in yourself:

1. Meditate.

2. Journal and make a list of the limiting beliefs that are separating you from being your higher self. This will slowly

start to reveal your inner program that is no longer serving you.

3. Do this first thing in the morning. I´ve found that in the first moments in the morning, my nervous system feels more neutral, so it's easier to bring new information rather than in the afternoon or night.

Do things that will keep your energy vibration high. This will attract high frequency experiences and people in your life.

The Matrix: Where the Game Is Held by Time and Space

Now that we are open to the idea of consciously exploring who we are as humans, it is vital to understand the playground. This playground, held by time (+) and space (-), also known as the 3rd dimension, is created from this polarity. It is in this physical dimension in which we can see this polarity from one perspective, from our *Iness*, which is equal to a specific focus point or consciousness: our Ego. This trinity can be seen with and through the third eye, which allows us to see the truth beyond the polarity.

That is why a human being is made from this trinity, as well: the spirit (vibration), the soul (energy), and the body (matter). It is essentially the same thing, vibrating differently, from the essence all the way to matter, as a way for the universe to understand itself through experience. This means there is only one reality, but in different ways of expression.

That is why, hacking the game reality is essentially about playing with this puzzle and creating coherence between these three aspects of the being: attuning your Ego with your soul and spirit. This is where real power comes from, because it will flow through your body technology like an engine, directed by your will and focus, to create a new and different reality in the third dimension, a reality that is equal to your specific vibration. So even if we are separating these three aspects of being human into spirit, soul, and body, they are not separate things — they are all connected through the same vibration, which is the Spirit: the Oneness, God, Universe.

It is in this playground where we are meant to experience every possibility with the task of aligning three realities in just one. That is why the third dimension is challenging since we are dealing with a whole fractal of emotions to eventually understand the experience. It is when we are not able to understand that we get stuck in the process, meaning that the chakras are not able to roll and move the energy through, manifesting physically in illness. It is here, in this game reality, that we come to understand who we are through experience.

Perceiving our body as technology, computer, or a vessel, can help us understand more about how to work with it. The body being the hard drive and the soul is the software (the program that goes inside the hard drive), and then wifi would be the spirit. Perceiving emotions as different perspectives in which we can experience the truth, the energy that makes the computer work through the chakras, being a consequence of that vibration.

That is why coherence is the most important thing in matter, because we are meant to align the three aspects of ourself within ourself, and that is when you find your own truth, your own perspective of reality.

CHAPTER 6

Our Story Is Our Most Magical Power

We assign meaning to our lives. What has been seen cannot be unseen. This is the power of consciousness. The power of consciousness applies also to the meaning you decide to give to things, which is equal to the story you are choosing to tell yourself.

By being the consciousness behind my powerful body avatar — the explorer in this amazing game reality —I became more aware and responsible of my inner dialogue and my perspective on things, including my past and the experiences that forged me.

The author Tony Robbins says that *there is no meaning to anything, but the one that we give to things*. It made me question, why do things have to mean something specifically? Why, when things don't go as we would have expected them to happen, they cannot mean that we are actually being blessed and aligned to greater experiences?

I chose to explore different meanings that felt more authentic respecting certain situations. I essentially became a child again. I then found myself changing the meaning of things in my past, because I knew I could. I was free. If I were wrong, I would have learned anyway, and would have at least explored life the way I wanted to. It felt right. This decision belonged to me. It didn't feel off or fake. I realized the greater story to be told was my own.

If we are not aware of the story inside our minds, we justify ourselves. We create a narrative around who we are. It all comes down to the following: If we don´t know who we are, we are going to be told who we are. That is why choosing our stories around our past, present, and future, is practicing our magic and mostly — living it.

We could be justifying the job that we hate, or the relationship that we are unhappy in, simply because our story justifies our predominant belief system, and it makes sense to think this way, because it has been the story that we have been telling ourselves for a while, even if this brings pain and hurt. Consciously or not, we can even protect our stories and fight for the idea of who we are, all the way to becoming victims forever. So as long as we don´t know that we are free to change the meaning to our past experiences and adapt the meaning into the story that is aligned to our higher self, the stories can be working against us, instead of for us.

The biggest change that I lived through, in choosing how to see differently from my past experiences, was the one associated with my core trauma. I would defend my misery and codependency through the pattern of living treason through my closest relationships, because I saw myself as a victim. I wasn't aware of the power this story had on my life. But what initially caused me pain and confusion, distrust and suffering, has now become one of my most magical elements.

The world is made out of stories.

What Story Are You Telling Yourself?

Once we accept, understand, acknowledge, and recognize ourselves as the creators of our experiences, we can redefine their meaning, and they can be used in our favor.

Be open to changing the story about your life all the time. You are a creation in process.

The only constant thing in life is change, so by defining and polishing your story, you are flowing with changes and blending them into your own story, rather than fighting them.

Listen to yourself: What is the story that you are continually telling yourself?

1. Ask and journal about what shifts in your narrative about yourself and a particular situation happening in your life, is what you can apply to add meaning onto the future you deserve.

2. Remember that nothing has meaning but the one you are giving. Is there something that you can change the meaning of, for the purpose of play and practice?

3. Be honest. Giving meaning to things that happen in your life doesn't mean avoiding what is a fact. You can change the interpretation of things, you can change how you feel about a feeling, but you can change only the inner experience behind the outer experience.

The process of creating has life for itself, and personally I believe that it is more fun than the outcome or the creation itself.

Living in the Present

Here are some questions I have asked myself and my clients: If I am creating something for my future, does this mean that I am not present or enjoying what I already have created, because I am constantly thinking about my vision? Or, if I am always envisioning a future, how can I also be in the present?

In creating something new, we need to be at peace and accept what we already have created for ourselves. As long as you reject or neglect your past self who created this present moment, you cannot create something different. Accept what you have created for yourself now, in order to move on, even if you are not in the place you would have wanted to be. Loving is equal to setting it free, and as long as you don't learn to love your present and who brought you to this (your past self), you cannot be a true creator.

Here is the simple solution that we can apply in this very moment in order to be both living in the present, and at the same time creating a future: feel complete certainty of where you are heading and what you are creating, because in this present moment you are aware of what you are feeling and thinking. This is equal to being present in love.

As long as you love yourself, you will choose the better option there is for you to create. As long as you love yourself, you will want to experience the best that you deserve.

Don't put yourself under pressure to achieve big things or to leave a legacy. If that makes you happy, great, because it can help you to express more of your unique frequency, but there is nothing *we really need to do. It is essentially expression and experimenting with who we already are.* Leave the specifics for this amazing future for a moment and focus on the feeling around this future that you are creating, whether it is achieving great things or not.

Visualize a screen in front of you, such as for a streaming service. Choose from a spectrum of possibilities of what you want to experience. Think of this platform as your life, as the reality game. You are choosing from different possibilities to experience yourself in this game reality all the time: the poor, the rich, the healthy, the successful, the victim, the confident, the artistic version of yourself, or, more specifically, different combinations of yourself.

These are all possibilities that you can experience, and it depends on how creative you want to be. Imagine the infinite realities you can live in. All the versions of you exist there, in the streaming service (The Mind), even if you believe they don´t, they are one button away, it is you who is always choosing (your mind). If you could choose between all of them, why would you choose something less than the best one?

Remember we are playing a game, so let´s play —

Step 1: You have chosen that one possibility that you know you deserve. Without needing to know how or when it will happen, you experience the feelings from this possibility while watching, seeing, hearing, smelling, tasting, and touching from that particular perspective.

Step 2: As the observer behind the avatar explorer, you have limited consciousness. You now choose to have faith and certainty by surrendering to the universal creative powers to weave this beautiful future for you.

Step 3: Shut your physical senses by closing your eyes. Begin to meditate. Enter the heart space. Tune yourself into the present moment and feel that possibility of being, where you're already experiencing it in the physical. It sounds paradoxical, but life is paradoxical. Do this from a place of gratitude, not lack or need. That is how we give life to this possible choice, by living it in the present.

Step 4: As if you already know the last chapter of a novel or the outcome of a movie, you know what you need to do to get there. You let it go, because you are already living it in the present.

This is the moment where everything starts making sense.

Certainty About Your Future

If you are certain that an amazing future is being woven for and through you, you are already a winner. You have hacked the game. Why? Because you no longer need anything. Not even that future. You are already experiencing it. Why would you want it if you are already there? Live it with all of who you are, you are already there. You have accessed the dimension of magic, you are existing both in the present and the future at the same time, both in the physical and the higher dimensions. You have aligned your body with the spirit and your soul.

Metaphysically speaking, we are applying the Law of Mentalism where we direct our mind. We know with certainty that the future that we deserve is the one that awaits us because we feel it, and if we feel it, we are there, and if we are there, we are no longer lacking that future. Essentially our work becomes the sustainment of this feeling, which is equal to becoming this new reality. If thoughts are the *electrical charge* in the Mind, and feelings are the *magnetic charge* of the Mind, it means that the thought or vision (+) sends the signal out and the feeling (-) in the heart draws the event or reality back to you. So the feeling of being in love with this vision of your choice, and loving who you have become and are becoming, and practice it 24/7, will cause you to stop reacting to people or conditions in your life. This means that the outer environment will cease to control how you feel and think, which is equal to ceasing being victims of the environment and to stop feeling emotions that separate us from our vision and dreams. Because even if we know what we long for but are not able to draw the experience back to ourselves, by being responsive to the environment, it's also weakening our magic. If we really practice changing the survival thoughts and emotions to elevated ones, practicing opening our hearts and mastering the skill of moving out of survival, the question comes to the following: What are we practicing feeling in this moment? And if it's not now, then when? Are we waiting for the experience to happen to change our mindset, or are we working from the place where everything is created and we are changing our mindset to create the experience? It all comes down to that.

Coherence, then, becomes that real practice: Your actions and thoughts are coherent regarding what is awaiting you (what you are focusing on feeling and thinking), and whatever happens to you that is challenging, you already know that you will be able to use it to your advantage because it is already leading you there.

This is the secret that I have discovered. Being in complete presence, certainty, joy, and unattachment, knowing and being deeply grateful for what is taking me there. This is what the Incas called 'the real gold.'

How can I actually know and feel this amazing future, and at the same time be in the present?

1. Return to your center anytime you're pulled out of it. Whenever you feel distressed or anxious, relax your physical body first, then your physical mind. From this centered space, tune to the frequency of the future that you are creating by living in it.

2. Remember you cannot create from stress, fear, guilt of judgment, but the opposite: You separate yourself from your dream since those emotions are not equal to the dream.

3. Practice feeling that future all the time. Ask yourself all the time, what are you practicing now? Are you being coherent?

Whenever I doubt myself, my capacities to experience something that I want or to create something that I want, I change the switch immediately and choose love and certainty instead. Why not? If it's really up to me, as I believe, then I want to choose the best and the most fun. For me, it makes complete sense.

Practicing Coherence

Within your body you can create a union between thought and emotion, which physically and energetically means that you are uniting the lower and the upper body in your heart. Just like the symbol of infinity, "∞," energy will start moving and expanding from the inside to the outer field.

Coherence is the most difficult and the most important thing that you ever have in the universe of the 3rd dimension, because coherence means to be aligned to the heritage of the spirit, the heritage of the soul, and the heritage of the body.

Let's practice coherency through these steps:

1. Create coherence. Emotions and thoughts have to be united. It is key for you to create a united frequency: Emotion (-) + Thought (+) = united vibration that comes back as a creation.

2. Practice coherency in what you say you are, what you say you will do, and act upon it. There is no worse lack of self-love when we know we have to do something for ourselves, and we don't take any action. You can practice in something small, like saying you are going to wake up earlier and actually do it, going to exercise, and actually doing it.

3. Creating from a state of lack (needing: I need this and I need that) will create more lack and more needs. You will find yourself talking about needs every day, even though you know that is not what you want.

4. Write a list with everything that you want to experience in your life, and become that.

Redefining Your Past

The idea of life as a game reality is not new. The original concept of the game reality — a *Game of Knowledge*, also known as *Leelah* — was created by enlightened sages in India between 2,000 and 5,000 years ago to help people change their lives, evolve, purify the mind, and reach one's full potential.

In Leelah, the player learns to free himself from the illusion

71

that has strongly entangled his personality and to see his life as a reflection of the macrocosm. It reveals an easier road to life goals and to happiness. The highest goal of the game is to free the human consciousness from the shackles of the material world and reunite it with the Cosmic Consciousness, aka *The Mind*.

The game helps the player realize desires, destroy prevailing and limited stereotypes, helps identify the obstacles to the realization of goals and to overcome them. The playing field are the situations, beliefs, challenges, in the players life.

As players of the game — behind the lenses of the avatar, and from the consciousness that is experiencing this game reality — we have chosen the best future for ourselves, which is equal to what we believe we deserve to experience. We look back to our past and redefine it, that is, free it. What seemed to be wrong, or what seemed as if should have never happened to us, now can be perceived as something that simply we needed to experience in order for us to grow and recognize ourselves truly.

How can I not love my past if I am able to create something from it? The thing is that even if we are not aware of it, we are creating all the time. We are beautifully condemned into working with our stories, into bringing new things into existence and into documenting moments through different forms that are simply expressing an inner reality. So even if we have gone through trauma and negative or not pleasurable experiences, we are free to redefine them by applying the right construction of our story that serves us.

I am already free, complete, and live in love. I don´t need politics, laws, society, or the world to tell me if being me is right or wrong. This power belongs to me only, because I know who I am.

Practice Redefining Your Past

If we truly believe we creators can change the story of our creations, we can redefine our past, even the most painful situations. Letting go of the past by redefining it is one of our most powerful tools. We construct a different order based on our experiences.

We start from the past, followed by the present, and lastly the future. But in this game, we are going to start the future, then past, and then the present.

By knowing (feeling) our greatest future, and aligning to it by tuning ourselves to the frequency of our choice, we can look back from that *already having and being* in a materialized form (the future), and see from the future's perspective towards the past (the present).

We can see that our past experiences were needed in order to have the present. We were already walking toward the future.

Let's practice the following steps:

1. Choose to see your past experiences, even the hardest ones, as a part of this amazing future that is awaiting for you and that you deserve. You can choose to see them as follows: These experiences had to happen to me, in order to place myself into walking the path into this amazing future that is already built for me.

2. Use everything to your advantage. Your wounds can be turned into stories, your emotions can be turned into energy, your tragedies can be turned into peak points in your life where you decided to be different and were shifted into becoming someone better.

3. Use your story to create an impact on the world. Every experience that you have been through is a resource and a tool in your life. By applying your system of currency to the world, by becoming useful to humanity, by knowing yourself and how you are useful to the world, you can generate more currency into creating more experiences for yourself.

The main universal law is the Law of Mentalism. By understanding this law, we can understand how the game is made. I strongly suggest exploring the Universal Laws to have a better idea of the truths that are out there in the game. These universal laws were written by Hermes, or Thot, King of Ancient Egypt.

The Law of Mentalism is that everything is made up of cosmic thought. If I want to have something, I should not think about what I want but think that I already am that. Because the universe will receive the feeling I want, which is in the future, the only thing that it will understand is the emotion in the future, and it will only create more future, but never the present. It will always create need but never reality. The Law of Mentalism says that I am the product of the Mind and that is why *I must become that mind to build realities.*

Let's apply the Law of Mentalism into the thought process:

1. Ask yourself and make your dominant thought process: Am I resonating with lack or with already having and being?

2. Align your mind to the Mind, by being and feeling that you already are that version of yourself that your heart is longing for.

3. Ask yourself: If in my mind I am what I think I am, then everything I see around me is what I am. Then, should I change my thinking or am I okay with the reality that I have created?

Asking what is the main reason behind what you think you want is key to understanding why to think or want to take certain actions. It is not probably the car or the experience itself, but the feeling that you believe comes with it. So the key is to focus on the feeling.

Let's focus on the feeling:

1. Ask yourself and journal — Why is it that you want this specific job or experience? If you say money or financial freedom, for example, that is perfectly okay. But I will continue to ask, Why financial freedom? You might say because you want to buy the house of your dreams. I will then ask you why you want the house of your dreams? And you will say to *feel peace and security for me and my family.* So, if you see, you are looking for financial freedom to *feel peace, security, joy, and share it with your loved ones* — not for the money or for the house, necessarily, but for what you believe it will make you feel.

2. Journal the main goals that you want to experience in your life and find the origin or the feeling linked to the outcome of having these experiences.

3. Now that you know the origin of the experiences you have decided you deserve to experience, by applying the law of mentalism, focus on the feeling. Can you feel peace now? Can you feel joy now? Can you feel freedom now? Can you feel secure now?

If you choose to apply the knowledge of the Law of Mentalism, and you know that you will receive good news and miracles because you decide to trust and surrender, then miracles will start happening: by the constant focused feeling on it. This is living in the dimension of magic, the positive expectation and the acceptance of what comes, because we will know how to direct any challenge that might come. It is to have a healthier association with the future, the one that we know we deserve. By redefining our past, we are redefining our present and our future. You will start to see clearer your strength and your individual path.

CHAPTER 7

Ego and Magic

Caring for the Explorer

Understanding the Ego as a tool, and not as an enemy, is also making peace of parts of who we are. The *I*, the individuality, the masculine energy within us that is focused outwardly, has a vital role in the exploration that we are living in this life. Sometimes we believe that being spiritual means believing that Ego is the enemy and that we should not let the Ego live within us. Although there is some truth behind this idea, it is not accurate. I believe Ego has been misunderstood, and we are not working with it as we should, because it can be the most amazing tool that we can use.

In writing *The Free Will Method*, I studied and researched everything that I could regarding the Ego, which is deeply represented by the will, and it resides in our solar plexus area. It is in this part of the body where our vital force is expressed outwardly, represented by a lion or a tiger — as you can see these beautiful animals, they are all about, being at their most magnificent. The ego wants to create, the ego wants to express its own and unique individuality, it is the consciousness behind it that will either use it to its most amazing, or will be used by the Ego. That is why each body moves differently, has different styles, different sounds of voice, finds pleasure in different ways and simply wants to experience life in its own way.

An unbalanced and excess of Ego is represented by what we see today in most societies: *I want this, I should have this, if they have that, then why don't I have it as well? Why him, and why not me?* Ultimately, the game reality is perceived only by the senses, and because there is a limit in the physicality, there is a belief that we need to fight to get what is limited. Also, the Ego can ask us to be someone we are not, as long as we are recognized by others as important, famous, cool, or worthy, because, again, we are living life from the outside to the inside. That is why the I AM, the balance and the co-creative friendship between the I and the **AM**, the balance between being and doing, will actually make us experience Ego in an incredible, resourceful way.

If it weren't for the Ego, we wouldn't be able to survive, because it is the individuality that will ask the consciousness to hunt for food and look for shelter in order to survive. It is in the Ego that we want to become better, to look better, to feel better, and to experience the experiences we know we deserve. It is in the healthy Ego that we believe we deserve amazing experiences and an amazing life — in contrast to having an unbalanced Ego, this could mean that we perceive ourselves as better than the other, or we perceive ourselves as less, and therefore, can become oppressive or submissive to others.

The Ego can be be a tool to focus our attention, to direct our actions and to create something in reality, or it can separate us from the world, make us believe that we are alone and alienated, making us believe we are someone that we are not, such as to have a deep attachment to an identity, a story, or a personality.

The Ego is my self-expression. It's how I experience the game reality. It has amazing tools and sensory perceptions that I enjoy deeply. I was constantly rejecting it and was too passive. I believed I had to take care of others before me. I realized I didn't create solutions, but problems. I was making decisions and acting out of fear and not out of love. I started to set my boundaries, saying no, cutting people off who didn't make me feel good, and started to answer to my needs and work on my physical body, my mind, feeling stronger, more confident and in love with myself more.

This gave me self-power. How can you know if you are living a life with unhealthy self-esteem?

1. Notice if you are being way too permissive into allowing things that don't feel good for you, although they can be good for others.

2. Practice saying no and expressing your needs. This could be from simply saying no to to a social event invitation, no to being touched, etc.

3. Practice thinking about yourself — your plans, what you really want and not what people expect from you, and act upon it. You should be your priority, even if that means letting other people down.

4. Stop feeling guilty when thinking about yourself. It is healthy and sometimes it is the best you could actually do in order to balance other relationships. Remember that if you feel good and balanced, you can actually give your best to other people and situations.

Thinking for ourselves and building healthy boundaries and a healthy ego are key to expressing ourselves without fear. Once we create a relationship and perspective with our Ego, we can use it to our advantage, instead of being used by it.

The Creation and the Creator

What is the difference between your creation and you, the creator? The game that we are all playing will bring constant challenges in our life. It will ask you to believe and to think that you are different from what you truly are. When navigating through these challenges, you will grow stronger, more focused, and wiser. Remember, without an opponent, there is neither real growth — nor a game.

The yoga concept of *siddhis* is the perfect example in which we can understand the difference between our creations and the creator. When I was in the Indian Himalayas, in the small town of Vashist, *Guruji* — or my guru —who accepted me as his *chara*, or disciple, shared with me a lot of knowledge that I consider as one of the most precious gifts I have.

We spent time together, sometimes in silence and sometimes he shared with me the stories about Shiva and Shakti, or about other

Babas (other gurus), and even how corrupted and power driven they could also become. We ate apples that grew in all the trees around his tree house in the mountains, sometimes we smoked *hash* and he would cook us the most delicious and simple foods. He would always repeat mantras such as *Om Namah Shiva* in everything he did, and he even gave me a secret mantra for my own spiritual initiation.

He explained to me what *siddhis* were and how, by becoming closer and closer to *samadhi*, as the main outcome of the yogic game, the state of the buddha or illumination, the challenges became harder. By this he meant that *siddhis*, the mystical and supernatural powers that can be attained through the practice of yoga, are also an ego trap, in which the yogi can get lost in the game by the attachment of these powers.

Siddhis are natural capacities that are awakened through rigorous spiritual practices such as yoga and meditation. In India, it is nothing rare to hear stories about yogis or gurus who walk over water, fly, become invisible or bilocate in different places at the same time. You can read the *Autobiography of a Yogi*, by Paramahansa Yogananda, to understand more about this lifestyle. *Siddhis* are considered as natural as any other human quality attained, because they are simply powers to control the self and the natural world, in which humans belong. Although they appear to be supernatural, they are actually accessible to all humans and can be explained in rational ways. They arise naturally when, through spiritual practices, emptiness and openness of the mind is realized.

The *siddhis* are divided into normal *siddhis*, simply aligning ourselves to the forces of the world that transform elements and *extraordinary siddhis*, which are the ability to open up for the truth that leads to realization and enlightenment, by bringing themselves to a state where their thoughts are in complete quiescence.

This can be achieved by any human being, as though a structure and practice is required. What magic seems to be out of this world, if you go to India with the gurus or to other ancient civilizations with shamans — this is not weird at all. It is something that is everywhere in their stories, their words, and, basically, their lifestyle, their nature: our own human nature.

In yoga, the *Patanjali sutras* known as the yogic bible written by the ancient *veda* and philosopher Patanjali, describe the process of attaining a range of different *siddhis* through birth, because some people are born already possessing spiritual abilities or powers due to their *karma*; but also through plants that can spontaneously trigger siddhis, and through the practice of yoga, mantras, and meditation. Although these powers have to be sustained by the player, due to the ability to use them accordingly; otherwise, they can have a counterproductive effect, and even be traumatic, since the right environment has to exist primarily to attain such powers.

My guruji explained how some gurus lost their way, or delayed their way towards the state of *samadhi* or illumination, when attaining these powers, these creations. As explained before, they were in *Rajas* state of being, since they started using their powers for show and to prove to others how powerful they had become. You can see this in the biography of Osho or other spiritual masters that accumulate so much power over people through their own practice, that they get lost in them and instead of guiding others, they start to use them to become more "powerful," and instead of creating more balance in the world, they start to create chaos and confusion.

This happens when the explorer of the reality game becomes attached to its creation or *siddhis*. We then become attached to the idea of being someone because we have conquered this material conquest or social status, and disconnect to our own creator. It is tempting, because we might get recognition, money, or other things that can cause confusion, distraction, and stagnancy.

When I found myself judging myself into not creating this or that, or comparing my creations to this or that, it made me feel frustrated, impatient, and even made me feel less deserving. It has been those moments when I have decided to come back to myself and realize that my creations are taking their own place and that the focus should always be on me, not on the outside world — because, honestly, most people are attached to their creations and how they look rather than who they are. They are anxious and conditioned by the outer circumstances, rather than the inner circumstances. So, remembering that it is not about the creation but by playing the creator role, gave me perspective and gave me a sense of freedom that I had not experienced before. Playing the creator role is to have fun and to explore, without attaching to anything.

Playing the Creator Role

By acknowledging ourselves as creators, we become conscious of creating out of nothing. It is the *Sattva* state of being. That is why comparing yourself should only be applied to your past self from the present self. If you are judging yourself due to your creations, you are creating separation. You are conditioning yourself from the order of out to in, rather than from in to out. The 'out to in' can bring frustration, depression, separation, and fear.

There is no one like you out there. You have a specific set of skills, resources, qualities, and dreams. Why would you ever compare yourself to others? Only when you are in a state of fear can you believe and let this comparison about not being enough, or not being good enough, sink into your energy field. This can bring frustration, heaviness, jealousy, and fear that is completely unnecessary. But the more you come back to your heart and forget about what everyone else is doing, the more fun and the greater you will become.

Here are some suggestions for having fun in creating:

1. Stop judging yourself based on the outcome of your creations, but focus on how you can polish your creating process instead.

2. It is the wealth system that you need to polish: What makes you different and what is your essence — how are you applying it?

3. Stop comparing yourself to other people's progress. You should not care about what other avatars or other people are doing. Remember, this is your game and focus should be on yourself.

It is easy to be pulled away from your center. This is something that the system wants. But if you solidify and crystallize this feeling inside you, no one can ever take you out of there. Remember your creations are your *siddhis* or yogic powers, so asking yourself if you are creating attachment to them can help you come back to your center:

- Ask yourself every day, am I connected to my creation as well as my inner creator? Creator is in the heart, as creation is in physicality.

By continually reminding ourselves that we are creators, we can see what we are creating in the present, which is all that it is. The whole point of being alive is to grow, learn to love, and to have fun in the process! Then why should we do something if it's not going to make us smile?

Be the change that you want to see in the world. I believe the world needs more innocence, lightness, and joy. What about you? Are there any attachments towards your creations, towards your powers, or towards your recognition through them? Are you ready to let them go, and go higher?

CHAPTER 8

Understanding Masculine and Feminine Energies

Since the heart is the place of union, where everything is created and unified, it is important to understand the two energies within us that create when they come together.

Masculine being the + (positive) aspect of our energies, and feminine being the - (negative). Masculine represents thought and feminine represents emotion. When together, + and - or masculine and feminine, they create a frequency made out of an emotionalized vision, creating something out of it. This applies to everything in our universe.

The illusion of separation of the physicality, which is the deep identification with our bodies and matter, has created a false belief of division between what is feminine and what is masculine. Regardless of the gender of the person, these energies are always present and are vital aspects of the creation process.

Masculine energy is highly focused on the outside. It is goal-oriented, driving outward energy. Masculine energy is represented by the *I* since its energy creates individuality. It allows the soul or you to separate yourself from God or The Mind and to stand alone, be a specific individual and explore the physicality from a unique point of view and experience. Masculine energy is the *I* that is the Ego or the explorer that experiences the experience, and it needs the feminine to create something with.

Feminine, on the other hand, can be perceived as a formless spirit, like an ever-flowing ocean, that needs direction of the masculine energy to manifest as a form in the physical. Together these energies create, and experience the whole from a unique, focused concentrated oceanic consciousness: You.

Although masculine and feminine energy are mostly perceived as opposites, there is a lack of knowledge of how to perceive these two energies, understand them, and use them to our advantage. Make peace with who you are and who you have been or not been, because this also means accepting specific parts within yourself. Once we start adding judgments like, *I am way too sensitive or too rational, I am too slow or too reactive*, but try to understand and integrate, we will be living in a state of separation, when we could be creating great things consciously.

Masculine energy creates individuality.

The fourth chakra is located in the chest, the one chakra out of the main seven chakras, that unites both the three upper chakras and the three lower chakras. Chakras are the energy vortexes, our human technology, that concentrate the emotions or information in the body, and create a kind of filter from which the body interprets the information received from the outside world. So the one in the heart space, the *anahata* (or "indestructible") chakra, is where these both energies become one: an united emotionalized vision, where they dance and create, also where the body is connected to the source, a dimension where you can live from love and in certainty, where fear and separation dissolves because love is above everything, and where you can start living life through unconditional love, compassion, and real freedom, which is that of being who you are.

You, by being in the body here on Earth, experience the body and the Ego through an individual self. The Ego is the avatar given or chosen by your soul when you come to explore this physical reality, and this Ego comes with a specific algorithm or qualities, such as a gender, a social structure, energy, and specific DNA structure. Therefore, everything physical is Ego too, it is the consciousness (you) behind the Ego that uses the Ego to either destroy or to create. The game itself, this game reality, is Ego. Our true selves are the observers behind the explorer or avatar (the mind) where this reality is explored. It is through focusing and directing (+) the oceanic source (-), in which we become amazing sailors of the wave tides in the ocean.

How to make peace with and start integrating your masculine energy?

1. Ask yourself if you notice constricting areas in your life. Are you pretending to be strong by avoiding feelings or acting like you don´t care or feel for something? Do you feel harshened up inside?

2. Ask yourself if you can see any focused and directed areas in your life. Are you able to focus and direct your intentions towards creating possibilities around your goals? Are you acting consistently and outwardly towards your vision?

3. Ask yourself if you can see healthy or unhealthy individualized areas in your life?

If you have a better understanding and relation toward your masculine energy, you will know how to balance it and how to use it to your favor.

Creating from a State of Masculine-Feminine Unity

The female energy is leading and inspiring, an oceanic flow, while the masculine energy is serving and protecting this flow.

The ancient yogis in India express the union of the female energy and the masculine as the goddess Shakti uniting with the god Shiva, coming together as one.

Shakti is feminine energy, the primal source energy, the flowing light, the oceanic formless spirit, the energy that has not yet been manifested, the inner aspect of things, the energy of oceanic fire that waits to be awakened by Shiva, or the masculine energy.

Shakti energy, also known as *Kundalini* or *the fire serpent*, lives inside us between the two lower chakras in our spine (the Muladhara chakra or perineum and Svadhisthana chakra or genital area). It is awakened by individual consciousness (focus and vision), and it is brought up to the heart by will and breath, a journey in which feminine oceanic fire cleanses, purifies, and transforms all the information in the spine through the chakras, from the tailbone to the crown, and awakens the divine within.

When the Shakti energy expands in the heart and finally flows up all the way through the throat or Vishuda chakra, passes through the third eye or Ajna chakra and finally reaches the crown or Sahasrara chakra, she opens the door in the highest point of our skull and becomes one with Shiva.

When Kundalini awakens by focused intention, she becomes aware of the movement inside her, of this oceanic fire that wants to play and experience, a desire to create form. The feminine energy represents God, the AM, home, and The Mind itself.

Masculine energy answers this call of experience and puts himself in service to manifest her in form and in matter. Considered as the mind, it is the outward-focused energy that gives form and shape to this oceanic fire feminine and directs her into a focused direction, which becomes a creation or expression in the physical world. It is this dance and cooperation of feminine and masculine energy that makes everything possible and creates magic around us. Without one or the other, or believing that these two energies are opposites, we will never be able to create a new reality in which the explorer can experience different experiences by changing forms of manifestation.

I really love this expression of the masculine and feminine energy, because practicing yoga and meditation is all about this connection that is meant to happen within us.

Changing our perspective into masculine and feminine energy over male and female gender or sex lets us understand our essence and nature of who we are. They are simply energies that represent the two aspects of all that is, of God or Universe, and they are not really opposed or dualistic — they are one, they are two faces of the same coin.

Feminine energy is the energy of Home and Oneness. It is the energy of Love and God. It is the energy of the primal source or the infinite ocean in which everything is made. The feminine energy does not differentiate or individualize, but by being individualized by the Ego or masculine energy, it takes form into creation.

Balance and healing are essential. I love that I am able to think about others and consider other people's needs. I understand how to take care of myself by not neglecting my needs as well, by also considering what is important for me even if that means letting people down. It all comes down to understanding our masculine and feminine energies! I was afraid of speaking my truth (my inner oceanic understanding), until I outwardly expressed it.

How to create from a state of unity instead of separation?

1. Ask yourself where there are divisions in your life. For example, I want freedom, but I cannot forgive this person. I want to be strong, but I am afraid to feel love. I only love what I understand. I accept this part of myself, but not this other part.

2. Ask yourself if you are ready to open your heart and live from the heart. This means being open to love anyone and everyone, starting with yourself. Are you ready to experience unconditional love, even if it scares you — even for those who have hurt you?

3. Can you see that unconditional love means being strong and vulnerable at the same time? Can you see the union of all things merging in the heart? What once seemed to be separate, becomes as one in the heart. It is paradoxical. I am. You are. Love is all. Creating from this space, makes you truly unstoppable.

The strongest I have ever been, has been when I have been the most vulnerable to feel everything that is, even though it is scary. So understanding about the I AM mantra and what it means, can help you put it into practice.

By understanding and perceiving the essence of masculine energy, its qualities, its objectives, we can balance this energy and use it to our advantage.

The Concept of 'I AM'

With a clearer idea on what masculine and feminine energies actually represent in our inner creative process, we are going to bring these two energies into a concept we can start applying now: I Am.

Even if we constantly repeat "I AM" in our lives — such as, "I am an architect," or "I am very hungry," or "I am here" — understanding the power of these words will help us connect to the creator inside of us.

Part of what disconnects us from our inner powers is that many important concepts remain abstract and far from becoming practical in our lives. Incorporation, and becoming — the alchemy within — light up this wisdom to be used and shared.

When we unite the masculine energy and feminine energy — the I with the **Am** — we simply become. We simply are. "I am magic." We apply the Law of Mentalism, the union between the mind and The Mind, the union between our individuality and our oneness. When the explorer's individuality is in constant co-creation with the oceanic source, we become unstoppable and real creators, we are creating from within, awakening the powers from within, creating things that appear to come out of nowhere, but they are really coming from the eternal Source.

Creating is our nature, which is why we are powerful and limitless. As long as we have hope and imagination, we will create different opportunities and solutions. We create from the abstract to the practical, from the feminine to the masculine, from the mind to the heart, so as long as we are constantly balancing both of these energies inside, we are uniting more and more parts of ourselves, becoming more solid and focused.

Passion is connected to the fire element. Passion makes us wake up in the morning and move our bodies. Passion is related to things that we love the most, things that can make us feel fire inside of us. That is why when you really don't like a job or you are bored in a social circle, you can feel tired and discouraged.

Once we have this spark — a dream or an invention — we can nurture it and give it form with our focus, our intellectuality and action, which represents the masculine energy.

Even if we are not defining this process from a feminine or masculine point of view, we can actually have a better sense of knowing ourselves and how we can balance them out. The unbalance can be manifested in procrastination. Feminine energy is calling you to bring more masculine energy into your life, or it could be the opposite: You want to create things and you seem to be forcing them into your own specific plan, with no flexibility or openness in flowing on towards other peoples opinion because you have a fixed image in your mind. Masculine energy, here, could be calling your attention into balancing your feminine energy and bringing more playfulness and flow, which are qualities of the water element: the oceanic fire of the feminine energy.

Becoming I AM comes down to becoming the creator. So you are more than an architect, you are more than any that you want to add into the I AM phrase. You already are.

In the I AM, the male and female come together and blissfully join their energies. One is needed for the other one to exist. They are two aspects of God, and therefore they are not really opposed, but two faces of one thing. In the masculine there is always the essence of the feminine, and in the feminine there is always the essence of the masculine, just as there is a white dot in the black and a black dot in the white in the ying- yang symbol. But in the course of history, this mystical unity of the masculine and feminine has been forgotten and these energies have become opposed to each other as black and white, from within and without.

I've mentioned life being a game. Whether you believe this is up to you, it works for me, because I can explore my full capacity of being, and it serves the purpose of expressing my idea through the imaginaries created in this book. It is through the exploration of the game reality, by being the observer behind the explorer, that I know that I am the energy of God or The Mind that is expressing itself through my mind, my individual avatar.

So how can we actually start applying the I AM meaning in a practical way?

- Practice being non-judgmental for 24 hours. Avoid placing

any quality like pretty or ugly, good or bad, not even to food, or to anything or anyone for 24 hours.

- Practice being non-judgmental for 7 days.

- Practice being non-judgmental as a state of being. It is the judgment that separates, and the non-judgment that accepts and experiences from a place of unity. It is then the heart state of being.

- Journal what you can see from the outside world as masculine energy. It could be related to politics, war, control, being connected to the outer world.

- Journal what you can consider from the outside world as feminine energy. It could be seen in nature, thriving alternative communities, being connected to the inner world.

- Journal and ask yourself what you can understand about yourself by perceiving these truths in the outside world. By looking out and looking in, can you see some connections?

The masculine and feminine energies depend on each other, and the balance between them is important. I believe that whenever we are at peace with ourselves and who we are and accept both feminine and masculine energies as complimentary energies instead of rivals, peace will manifest.

Start practicing the becoming of I AM as a new state of being:

- Study the masculine and feminine energies in your chakras. Ask yourself how to balance the three lower chakras that are feminine energies expressed as belief and emotion. Do you feel disconnected from your lower body? Do you lack passion, pleasure?

- Ask yourself if you can balance the three upper chakras that are masculine energies expressed as vision and thought. Do you feel disconnected from your upper body? Do you lack concentration, decision making, focus?

- Balance the left side and right sides of the brain. The right side is feminine, connecting to the parasympathetic nervous system, creativity and expression, and the left side of the brain is the masculine energy that connects to the sympathetic nervous system, survival, rationality, and structure.

- Can you see that being in survival mode, stress mode, excessive masculine energy releasing cortisol and adrenaline all the time, keeps people from sleeping and being connected to their bodies?

- Practice yoga, meditation, breathwork, pranayama and conscious relaxation to activate the feminine energy.

- Practice exercise, will power, routines, taking action, and healthy competition sports to activate masculine energy.

- Read *The Free WIll* Method to understand deeply about the chakras and the balance dance between masculine and feminine energies towards creation.

By playing and integrating these two different and complementary energies together into your individual, creative, personal and external life, you grow more sensitive when you feel out of balance and how to come back to balance. I AM essentially means aligning yourself with the spirit, in which the real power is manifested.

If you are working on creating a change in the world, the rational and most effective thing to do would be to balance your inner world first, instead of hating, judging, or creating more separation on the ones that are wrong (by judging). You cannot create a real change by behaving the same as the ones that are. The only thing you can really do is to become and anchor the new into your body.

CHAPTER 9

Humans Are the Greatest Source of Power

Our bodies are generators of energy. As long as your soul is connected to your body, your body lives, and whenever your soul leaves the body, the body starts dying. Imagine the body is like a spaceship literally moving and exploring the physical reality through the directions of your soul. Your consciousness is making the decisions whether to go east or west, whether to talk to this other avatar or the next or whether to interact with any kind of element. Your body's a spaceship where your soul is the key that activates its engines.

Exploring Sacred Geometry

Body = spaceship.

As any other vehicle, our spaceships need to be maintained.

The body has seven energy vortexes, or chakras, that keep things working. Whenever there is an imbalance or a blockage in any of these energy vortexes, the hormonal glands will deliver signals to the consciousness or explorer (you) in order to fix it. If the explorer is too distracted by the game reality, these signals eventually grow into painful and solid expressions in order to be seen — tumors, cancers, or other physical manifestations of unbalance.

The hormonal glands in the body are connected to the chakras or energy vortexes, and the ones that associate the outer information to create thoughts and emotions. The hormonal glands produce the hormonal chemicals such as adrenaline or serotonin, based on memory patterns, and programming. The more you keep your body as light and balanced as possible, the more clarity you gain, and transmute the energy that blocks the conduction of power in the spaceship.

Like a spaceship or vehicle, the body requires a commander to direct its course. This commander, found in the Ajna Chakra or the third eye (the all-seeing eye), has a vision and a route, directs the energy by building images and words, and finds solutions that hold a vibrational frequency for the vehicle.

The Anahata chakra, found in the heart, is the one energetic vortex capable of transforming the electricity directed from the third eye, and the solar plexus, representing the sun and the individuality of the spaceship, but also it represents the capacity to generate the energy required for what the explorer is asking. This center, also known as Manipura Chakra, brings out the light from our centers, from our vital force, toward the world and the universe. In the solar plexus, our Ego sits and works as an output, reflecting the light of the sun from the body, showing how beautiful the spaceship is with pride and self-love.

This output refers to the information or emotion that is passed from our spaceships back to the universe, just as a software controls the passing of information to a computer. We are the universe expressing itself egocentrically in a given space and moment through our magical tools called bodies, and the whole point is to express the love of the universe and to grow from this love through art, a product, a service, through singing, kissing, hugging, exploring, and essentially through experiencing this reality.

By understanding the potential of our incredible machine, and keeping the right functioning of the chakras or energy vortexes, we can bring together a non-physical vehicle called *Merkaba* within our energetic field. Merkaba means *chariot* or *vehicle* in Hebrew. It is a shape made of two intersecting tetrahedrons spinning in opposite directions, creating a three-dimensional energy field. We can activate this vehicle of light around our own body with practiced meditation and breathing techniques. This sacred geometry vehicle can transport our consciousness to higher dimensions, which I can define as the true capacity of our bodies when understood and activated accordingly.

We can start to see our bodies as sacred, because they are. They are the vessels of our light, and it is vital to let go of everything that is keeping us from activating our full potential.

We are able to tap or exist into different dimensions through our emotions. When we talk about chakras, we speak of dimensions as well. We all have seven main chakras in our spine, connected to seven vital hormonal glands (the ones that are segregating information and chemicals that create emotions). And each chakra represents seven different dimensions from which we can learn about ourselves. Chakras are spinning wheels of energy located along your spine. These energy centers are all related to particular life-themes.

The chakras are to some extent part of the material reality, since they are related to specific places in your body, but they are not visible to the physical eye, so you might say they linger between spirit and matter: They bridge the gap. They are the point of entrance for spirit or soul consciousness (-), enabling it to take physical form (+) and create the things that you are experiencing in your life.

Specific emotions manifest in specific chakras, and in specific parts of our body. Let's look closely at our energetic vortexes that represent the electrical fields in our body and what laws of the universe can be understood through them:

Maintenance and High Vibrations

How can I start focusing on what I want and keep my vibration high?

Here are some examples that you can follow:

1. Stop perceiving what you no longer want from life. Unfollowing certain people that trigger low vibration thoughts such as comparison, separation, hate, and anger.

2. Make your environment a product of your creative process.

Pictures of the body you deserve, the house you deserve, the trips you deserve, affirmations in your bathroom mirror, etc. Surround yourself with people that feed your inner fire, instead of questioning it and make you question it.

3. How strong is the dream that wakes you up? Is it truly what you long to experience? Make a practice out of strengthening the image of that dream.

4. Dare to see the future that you want and deserve, without thinking about others.

5. Receive and choose that everything that happens to you, you justify it at your best. Remember that what happens to you doesn't happen to you, but happens for you.

When you understand how to control your consciousness by exercising your power of will, you will see that you can choose a different consciousness than what's around you. And you will notice that your environment will begin to change as a result.

It is key to understand that from self-love arises creativity. You cannot create from the most subtle energy (the highest of all) if there is a part of you that you deny or judge yourself, if there are other people's opinions that you let block you. You have to be in balance to create, since, remember, you are the one who gives meaning to things.

Here are ways to become more responsible in the creative process:

1. Take responsibility for your healing.

2. Step out of victim mode.

3. Polish and practice your emotionalized thinking. Your creative process can also be perceived as the union of belief with vision.

4. Ask yourself if you have any incoherence in your vision and belief. Change your perception of this emotion so it comes aligned to your vision.

Our human technology, as a conductor of light and power through the chakras, is a map for understanding where there can be blockages holding us back, or where we can potentialize this conduction. Since each chakra is connected to a different dimension and state of consciousness to specific emotions and information, the Merkaba or spaceship of the soul, can be accessed through consciousness of who we are by the continuous balancing and polishing of our bodies through the intention and vision of the mind.

Know more about your energetic centers, dimensions, and the laws of the universe:

The chakras are the point of entrance for spirit or soul consciousness, enabling it to take physical form and create the things that you are experiencing in your life. Dimensions are a measurement of points of view (+ and -), meaning that every dimension is a measurement of only one thing.

The Muladhara Chakra

The first chakra is located at the base of the spine, specifically in the perineum, extending to the genital area. This chakra regulates our connection with the body and the physical plane, our basic and primitive instincts, especially that of survival and protection. It also governs our passion and our relationship with material possessions and work.

It represents the first dimension, the measurement of the The Mind, or God. Invites us to understand that everything is only one thing. The same thing can be seen also from two perspectives — positive (+) and negative (-).

The Sacral Chakra

This chakra is located four fingers below the navel, it has an influence on the nervous system and on body temperature. It harmoniously regulates the body, mind and emotions. It is related to sexuality and creativity, it controls the ovaries and testicles that are responsible for producing hormones involved in reproduction and responsible for causing changes in mood.

It represents the second dimension, + and - create the polarity of these perspectives of unity, called time and space. Through time and space, unity will be expressed.

The Manipura Chakra, or the Solar Plexus

The manipura chakra is the seat of the will. It is the center that focuses your energy into physical reality. It is the chakra that is connected to issues of creativity, vitality, ambition, and personal power. THE EGO and the WILL are closely related to each other. The faculty of the will enables you to focus on something, either without or within. Your perceptions of reality, of both yourself and others, are greatly influenced by what you want, by your desires, often intermingled with fear.

Master the energies related to control, manipulation, domination, trust and self-respect. Topics related to power conflicts, feeling powerless, inability to digest, swallow, or tolerate situations or people and being able to express anger in a healthy way. The will of the mind aligns itself with the will of the spirit in this center, becoming POWER, a word that comes from the Latin *potere*, which means to be capable of doing anything we want to. If the person feels strong love for his body and intends to keep it healthy, this center is open and self-acceptance will manifest itself on a physical level as bodily health. Excess weight in general is an indication of the malfunction of this center, especially when there is prominence and acidity in the abdomen area.

It represents the third dimension, when time and space collapse, creating the third dimension, which is unity. So it is basically the unity starting at itself and experiencing itself. This dimension is connected to the 6th dimension, where we get to experience what is being designed from that perspective: what we see, imagine, dream: the potentiality of creating realities within this game.

The Heart Chakra, or Anahata Chakra

The heart chakra is the seat of the energy of love and oneness. The heart carries energies that unify and harmonize. When you draw your attention to this center for a while, you may feel warmth or something opening up. It is located in the chest and represents the central point of the chakra system. It is the chakra that bridges the gap between the three lower (material and -) chakras and the three upper (spiritual and +) chakras. It represents the beauty of balance, the seat or throne of the soul that is what gives life to the body. It is considered the center of love because it allows the ability to give and receive from the heart, selflessly and unconditionally.

When this chakra is truly open with consciousness, we can experience unconditional love, as it is related to feelings and not to emotions, so that in the opening process and in those whose mission has to do with learning from the heart, the emotions will be purged and purified. It corresponds to the thymus gland, which in addition to being part of the endocrine system, is part of the immune system, responsible for defending the body against agents that cause stress diseases.

It represents the fourth dimension, which is the frequency in which the experimentation of oneness is happening, meaning time itself. It is basically how many times things happen and its repetitions. Basically, it is the *process* of the experience. As the oneness starts to spin, that spinning is the fourth dimension.

The Vishuddha Chakra, or Throat Chakra

The Vishuddha chakra is located in the center of the neck in the middle of the clavicle bones. Considered the center of communication, it symbolizes the expression of the inner truth to the outside, allowing the manifestation.

It represents strength and rigor, the desire to receive, courage and discipline, the desire to give, and complacency. It is also a center of sound and vibration next to the sacral chakra, it is a center of creative energy. This power center is the entrance to the miraculous, mystical and mysterious, since it connects us with the condition of space and time so that something can exist, that is: the beginning of the process of manifestation that involves the word.

We activate this chakra when we stop blaming others for our own vital deficiencies and dedicate ourselves to creating what we need and want. If the person has chosen a profession or occupation that allows him to use his talents and abilities, finds it exciting, allows him to fulfill himself and give the best of himself to others, then this center will be in full prayer.

The person will be professionally successful and will receive support from the universe to nurture himself as he will be exercising his potential through his creative capacity.

It represents the fifth dimension, the awareness of that spinning, where all the data that you are living is recorded.

The Ajna, or Third-Eye Chakra

The Ajna Chakra, or third-eye chakra, *the designer*, is considered the center of telepathy, clairvoyance, intuition, the understanding of our dreams and the recognition of our vital issues, as well as the vision of life, intelligence, and inner wisdom.

Physically this chakra governs the pituitary or pituitary gland, the master gland that controls all the other glands mentioned below in the following chakras. It represents understanding and wisdom, which together make up knowledge.

When we move from the fifth to the sixth chakra we are beyond the natural elements and have gone through all the transformations of our ordinary experience that are encoded by earth, water, fire, air, and ether.

This is the chakra of mastery and it is here that we achieve total integration of ourselves. It is here where *Ida* (-), *Pingala* (+) and *Sushumna (central nervous system)* energy channels meet, where the three rivers of our energy are integrated into one. It is the eye with which we see the truth, the two physical eyes give us dimension in the material world, but it is the third eye that gives us the capacity for vision, the depth and the dimension of the subtle worlds. Its function is to see the invisible and know the unknown, it is the center of direct connection with the infinite source of wisdom.

It represents the sixth dimension, meaning that once we are aware of our human technology, we can transform it into something different. We can use the awareness of the spinning of the fourth dimension, the experience in the third, and the polarity of the second, to transform the first dimension. Essentially, from this perspective is where we design what we are creating and experiencing in the third dimension, or planet Earth, as human beings.

The Sahasrara — or Crown Chakra

Through the Sahasrara chakra, or crown chakra we are linked to the reason of all Being. Total integration of heaven (spirituality) with earth (material).

It is the integration of our whole being: physical, emotional, mental, and spiritual. It represents the crown of the kingdom, the highest of divine emanations, one of the spheres of consciousness closest to the light of the creator. It controls the pineal gland considered as the exit door of the soul. The secretion of this gland is not constant, and the appropriate stimulus for it to occur is darkness.

The gland is rich in a derivative of serotonin and melatonin, a compound endowed with psychoactive properties, that induces visions that refer to inner travel. It is the exit and entrance door to return to the physical body in astral travel. When this chakra is open and in balance, the person often experiences its spirituality in a very personal and exclusive way. This spirituality is not defined dogmatically, nor is it expressed in words; it is rather a state of transcendence from mundane reality to infinity.

It represents the seventh dimension, since you now know you can transform oneness or The Mind, you become enlightened because you understand that you are of God, and it is you who is transforming your own reality. It represents the vibration of sounds that cover the entire universe. It is the resonance, the vibration of the understanding of the whole.

When that expansion from the seventh dimension gets to converge to itself, it creates the 8th dimension, which is eternity. Every being is living everything and you can perceive every timeline, every possible reality, which brings you to the complete understanding of every one of the parts, which is the 9nth dimension. This is the Divine, taking you to the oneness again.

So essentially, it is a recreation of itself once again and again.

Know and Balance Your Chakras. Use Them as Allies.

To understand and study ourselves, we are able to know how we can create constant balance inside and be less reactive to the outer world.

Chakras connect us inside and when balanced, they activate all of our potential by expanding our energy into a perfect sacred geometry called Merkaba. Kundalini flows through us and we start awakening different qualities, called *siddhis* (yogic powers) in the yogic language. We will be talking about *siddhis* further in the book. Once in power, yogic power or powers are attained through your practice. These powers can be the capacity to focus on one thing, to concentrate into your vision, for example, and the capacity to create an emotion, essentially: to create miracles from a state of being.

You are not a product of our environment, but the environment is a product of yourself. So sometimes it is key to isolate yourself from a known world, as I did, and move somewhere else where you can explore yourself differently.

Because of the law of mentalism, you are now conscious that what is around you is a creation of your old self, and once we start thinking and feeling something different, your environment will start changing. Sometimes moving away from a specific stressful environment that is contracting is the most efficient way to tap into our inner world and find clarity. That is why retreats are called retreats, because they literally mean retreating yourself from a known place and moving into another, so you can create a different world by changing your perception of it!

What If We Used All Our Power?

What would happen if we used all our power? What happens if we embrace our full capacity of being?

Before we do that, we need to know that we are able to become our own powerful and unique expression of God. If we really are limitless souls, an expression of God playing the game of reality, that means that we contain everything within ourselves, all the information in our DNA. This means that we are stars and suns inside skin and bones, and we are meant to shine and to explore and express our true self, our true beauty — it is to express God itself within us and through us.

But if we have forgotten this, the conduction that brings the life force into our bodies would not work and could even be debilitating, as we are completely focused on the outer world and completely conditioned by it. I call this to have a cold spirit, an effect of our unconscious choices of living for others and to make choices that make sense to others. It is simply ignorance of who we are and therefore, the disconnection with our power, the power that we are constantly giving away and not even knowing how we are giving it away.

As a machine, our body has the most perfect technology of all. It is made to be attuned to the Source, to be a bridge from the divine plane to this one — it is made to experience love and the pleasures through the physicality of planet Earth. It is meant to function as a vessel of our souls and the spirit, it is meant to be a great source of power since the souls are extensions of the power itself of The Mind or The Creator of it all. Whatever name or label you have for *everything that is* doesn't matter, because as long as you are aware of the essence behind the concept, you will understand and make use of what I'm writing here.

The concept of power itself has also brought confusion into the world. Power is *the capacity of doing something*, but it is often associated with the capacity of doing something through *having or owning*. It is the belief that having power is gained through having more land, minds, resources, and money. That is why the fight for power has become our present reality, because of the lack of awareness of individual inner power. If humans really knew, as individuals, their own creative capacity and how powerful they are, they would use their power to create what their authentic self longs for. But by ignoring this, they give away a continuous and constant leak of this power to the ones who actually understand this and don't want others to awaken to this idea by the story that they are constantly telling.

True power resides within us, and it doesn't need anything but awareness. True inner power — magic — is the capacity to do more and more with less and less until eventually you can do everything with nothing. Just as in nature itself, no two flowers are identical, no two human souls are identical. Therefore, by being who you are, you are already contributing to one another, like nature does by itself. You have a unique frequency that expresses itself through a unique form and way. You would be using your powers to create your own magical reality, without the need to fight for it, because, just as with lions and trees, the real power is confidence of knowing you have the power to do what you need to do when you need to, instead of constantly be proving yourself to others as to be perceived as powerful. A lion doesn't need to prove anything — he knows who he is and lives by it.

Lao Tzu, the Chinese philosopher and founder of Taoism 571 a.c, said: *He who knows others is clever, but he who knows himself is enlightened.* As long as you know that you are divine and that you hold all the love and power within, you will live according to who you are.

Your Capacity for Feeling and Emotion

Feel your own capacity for producing a feeling and an emotion.

You can produce energy just as a hydroelectric power generator does. Consider rivers: The movement of the current in rivers has the power to create electricity. Humans don't need much to create. We barely need the basics to subsist in a very healthy way, we need far less than we think. As long as we have sunlight, a simple diet and sleep, we are basically set. But our amazing Ego is the one that is exploring this reality, so, of course, as an explorer it wants to experience different things, which is amazing and exciting.

Knowing who I am has made me feel free and powerful. I stopped needing other people's energy or outer things to feel a certain way. I stopped expecting others to recognize me as I already knew who I was. I chose to recognize myself and see myself.

Knowing who I am has made me understand my resources and my power. So now I know how powerful my thoughts, emotions, words, and energy are in my body, in this particular moment in time. Emotion can be interpreted as *energy in motion*, the fundamental basis of which is an emotion means to *move*. Something that is in motion — E = out, Motion = movement. Over time, we recognize it as a *feeling.*

Emotions are one of the most important things that the universe has created because emotions are the portals toward every dimension.

Let's look at your relationship with emotions:

106

1. Journal, and make a list of the strongest positive or negative emotions that are mostly recurrent to you in one year. This could be rage, love, anger, guilt, happiness, etc.

2. Journal and make a list of the most common positive or negative emotions you experience during a common day. This could be sadness, happiness, fulfillment, anger, etc.

3. Practice meditation based on the book *Heart Center Living*, by Pamela Kribble.

Channel Your Power Into Creating

Whatever life throws at you, practice the certainty of the future that awaits you (focused vision). Once you are aware of this creative certainty state of being, *nothing happens to you, but it works for you* to keep on living in certainty.

You can channel your power into creating. No one but you owns that power. We are magicians and we become in the expression of God once we stop being victims of possible futures.

Emotions are electrical pulses within our body and movements of energy or waves in the inner sea. A feeling is something that is acquired, and an emotion that was assimilated to last over time and has created a constant energetic state. This means that we can achieve a desired state of being from the constant energetic pulse conducted to an end.

It is important to understand the close relationship between mind and emotion (the I and the *AM*) since both need each other.

What we feel inside is a reaction of internal energy from external impulses, therefore, the way I can change the reaction before it reaches me is as follows: *without modifying the outside world, but by changing my perception of the outside world*.

Our Emotions and Our Source

We could say that the body is the ship, and consciousness is the sailor in the third eye who transforms the waves through the heart and through the solar plexus.

If we don't understand something or how to handle it, it can be difficult to transform it and make it something useful. But if you learn how to change your perspective, and polish it constantly based on your focused vision, then you will be able to harmonize the external impulses before an emotion is created. By changing our perspective about the world, and about who we are, from the story we are telling ourselves, we become masters in sailing the sea.

Let's put in practice the power of imagination:

1. Remember a moment where you felt recognized for achieving something.

2. Now that you have identified this moment, feel the feeling or emotion in the body. Can you sustain this vibration as long as you can by keeping focused on it?

3. Meditation

Through practice and consistency, we can master bringing physical particles together and create realities.

Making an Emotionalized Thought

We know we are the greatest source of power in ourselves. How can we start to apply it and direct it in a systematized and practical way? Think when you have gotten angry, or have experienced rage or jealousy or even fear. Think about when you have felt the deepest love or think about a loved one that you feel lots of love for. If you think about it, what you are doing in that moment, far away from being "good" or "bad" emotions, is that you are generating energy from associating something in your mind into an emotion.

Since your body is plugged to the universal Source by an invisible but strong string, this string is communicating both ways all the time. Your body is made to experience emotions, because in other dimensions where your soul doesn't have a body, there is no way to experience emotions since emotions belong to the physicality. So you, as a creator, are constantly receiving and perceiving electric pulses, called emotions, that send a vibration back to the universal source, and that vibration, if consistent, comes back in matter to the physicality.

Creating a thought by itself, with no emotion, will not create anything. It is the emotion from the thought that will move the water inside of you, and create waves that access the subconscious mind, or The Mind, which is the way that the universe receives this information and responds or reflects back as a creation. Since everything is energy, an infinite ocean made from infinite subtle currents, that contains everything that is, there is always a constant creation and attraction, even if you are aware of it or not.

Free will applies here in a sense that we can start choosing different thoughts, that will create different emotions, that if repeated strongly, will eventually become a feeling, and a feeling is a state of being, and that state of being will materialize by the mind. It all comes back to observing our thoughts and choosing different thoughts that now represent who you really are and the future that you deserve.

Start to observe and not to judge your thoughts through practicing meditation. This will reveal the story that you are telling yourself and the emotions around it. You will be able to change it accordingly.

The responsibility of the creation of thoughts will bring impeccability of thoughts, words, and new emotions. You will start choosing what emotions to generate, what power to generate, and through consistency, repetition, self-suggestion, and basically habits and lifestyle, you will start to create a different external reality that resonates with the new inner reality.

Creating an Emotion

As much as any other talent, everything requires practice and consistency. I think that the most important thing is that you have an idea of how it works for you, because maybe you can find a more efficient way that feels true to you. For me, it has become easier because I have already practiced so much that my mind and body are more sensitive to vibrations and I am also more connected to my emotional body. I have worked on my individuality and learned that my inner light needs to be fed every day by my passions.

The ability to create a feeling is to consciously intend to unite a thought (+) with the force of emotion (-), and the force of this emotion is fed by your inner fire. You use your free will to practice the emotionalization of a thought. You direct this fire and inner energy towards your vision.

Here are some suggestions for understanding the process of emotionalized thinking to create and direct new thoughts.

1. Read *Electric Living*, by Kolie Crutcher. Remember that by understanding how the law of attraction works, we can find it easier to use it.

2. Practice your free will. Make a decision of what you want. You can start with something small, like something you want to experience today. It is important to practice decision making because that will bring clarity on bigger decisions. The universe doesn't measure or judge something as too big, too wild, or too much. You do.

3. Keep your inner fire lit by feeding it with your passions, small or big, and by choosing your vision — practice the emotionalization of it through meditation. This process is also known as *incorporation*.

What happens when we start practicing and start having results? Naturally, we start to become more responsible in our power because now we know that we are creating something out of it.

Polishing Your Power

I believe that power requires responsibility. If we already know and start understanding about ourselves being sources of energy and able to create and attract pretty much anything that we deserve, then, of course, we will start wanting to polish what we are attracting.

Polishing means finding our mindful intentions, but also our perspective on them, so it is coherent to what we love the most.

How can I polish my power?

1. Polish by bringing more clarity and detail in your intentions and visions constantly, as well as your beliefs, as well as your perception of things. The more you know yourself, the more

you know what you want and deserve.

2. Meditate every day and practice your free will power every day. You will be impressed on how things start aligning by being focused and determined.

3. Focus on the feeling of your vision and feel it constantly. Is it peace, is it fulfillment? Is it happiness, freedom, love?

4. Ask yourself if your choices make you feel more connected to the world. This can reveal your true intentions.

Practice will make you a master of your own creative process. Each one of us has different ways of creating. This means that you can follow methods that can definitely work and support yourself, but the one that will work the best for you is the one that you discover is your own, on your own rhythm and way.

Put in practice your state of being:

1. Ask yourself constantly (place an alarm in your phone every 30 or 60 min) what you're attracting now. The answer will be: the story you are telling yourself in that precise moment and the emotions surrounding it, and the feeling that comes out from this story. Change it by standing up, by taking a shower, by simply moving your body, clapping your hands or saying something out loud: *I Am an incredible magician.* The idea is for you to come out of that state of being and to recondition yourself to that.

2. Solidify the right story. Whenever you find yourself telling yourself the story that is not consistent with the life you deserve, on the left side of a piece of paper, write the wrong story and then transmute it or change it to the right story on the right column. Do this as much as you need to, anytime you catch yourself talking as your old self.

3. Have a journal with you at all times. Writing on a piece of paper has proved that you can organize your thoughts and bring clarity. So the more you write, the more you will be able to bring clarity inside, and, therefore, tap into the right story until it is completely solidified.

By understanding in deeper and specific ways, the power of creating an emotion, the power of our physical bodies as water bodies, and believing in yourself and the creator of this amazing process, you are pretty much opening a channel between The Mind to the physical reality, through your mind. This means that you can create and transmit the vibration that is aligned to the future that awaits you, and attract it there.

Becoming a Magnet

Our bodies are generators of energy, energy that comes from our souls and the energy that is all around us. Science and metaphysics explain that the space where the smallest particle lives, in any kind of matter, cannot be measured, nor is it fixed. This invisible and always-changing space is what weaves everything in the world together. It is the spirit in which everything has been and is being weaved.

A lot of people are looking to achieve higher dimensions and states of consciousness. I used to look for this promise of ascension. But my most valuable learning through my whole spiritual process has been acknowledging my humanity and choosing to work with who I am in this present moment. Instead of believing that being human was something that shouldn't, now I have chosen to completely embody my human body, made essentially of mud: water and earth. It was this realization that has brought me to write this book, because I have understood that there is nothing more powerful in this moment than assuming my task as a human, understanding what it is a body and an Ego, and working with these as tools, rather than obstacles.

By learning about the sixth and third dimensions, I came to understand that it is here, in the physicality, in the third dimension, in this reality game, where the beings of the sixth (a different perspective of who I am in the third), come to experience and explore a specific perspective of the oneness. So instead of looking to leave or judge being human as something less enlightened, the game and all of its opponents — the politics, the tricks, the limited beliefs — now I use them as enhancers of my own power since they are a great source of power or emotion. Accepting being a human and embodying that with all that I can, is realizing that I am a creator, and as a creator, emotions are needed since they make things move. So essentially, we either are trapped in emotion or we create with emotion.

By going inside the body, and understanding that there are thirty-three vertebrae in the spine, which hold the chakras, holding the spirit, which makes these chakras spin.

As I explained before, the hormonal glands are connected to the chakras, the ones in charge of interpreting the information and creating emotions, so by the awareness of how the chakras are balanced, basically, we are learning how to work with the emotions, rather than be conditioned by them.

The + and the - energies, which create this whole spinning inside of our bodies, will finally unite in the heart. The + energy, related to the *I* or *Father*, is the search for light, as is the - energy, related to the **AM** or *Mother*, is the search for grounding.

Being grounded on Earth, *being Earth*, water and earth, which equals into *being human*, and at the same time, allowing for the light to come in, to embody our Ego, our *Iness*, will eventually lead to alignment of the Ego with the spirit, which allows the real power to happen, the inner power — the alignment of + and -, becoming I AM, or in other words: embodying the Ego or bringing heaven to earth. This is a possibility in any human being, it is a spiritual process, the one which is also known as the Christ energy.

The body becomes a magnet by running a current down and up the spine, uniting in the center or heart, to produce an electromagnetic field, by releasing energy from the first three centers to the brain and back. As creators, as it is in our nature, we co-create different realities with the spirit, and we essentially acknowledge ourselves as humans, as explorers.

It is the moment when we start to become aware of our human potentiality that we can transform our three main human pillars, which are sex, food, and sleep.

These three pillars are key and connected to our mind, since food (energy), reproduction (sex), and sleep (regeneration and integration of information and energy) allow our cognitive and thinking capacities to function, so we can design different realities for ourselves. So that is why it is very important not only to accept our human needs, but also to love them, so we can transcend them and not be conditioned by them.

These three needs are connected to our lower chakras, our (-) or feminine earthly emotional aspect. Sleep is connected to the Muladhara or root Chakra, sex is connected to the Svadhisthana or sacral Chakra, and food is connected to the Manipura or solar plexus chakra. It is when we start using our WILL (connected to the third dimension and manipura chakra) when we start to direct our power, to create form with these emotions, to start acknowledging we are also gods within our humanity, that these three needs start to become tools. This is another way of understanding, not only our human potential, but how to bring the light to what before was only ignorance.

Where from the body am I creating? Here, I am addressing the heart chakra, which is found in your chest and linked to the thymus gland, the seat of the immunological system. Since most people are living from an ego-state consciousness or in a fear-based survival state, having the heart chakra closed is something that naturally happens, because it prevents us from feeling, being empathetic or compassionate towards ourselves or others. As long as our hearts are closed, we tend to take things too personally or hold stuck emotions like sadness, resentment, and anger for ourselves and others, and this keeps us from living life fully, but also it keeps us from being able to create a feeling. The general idea and belief about the heart is the ability to feel things, to love and being open, which in a survival environment is considered foolish, even a weakness, but also reckless.

I chose to open myself to different kinds of therapy, but the most effective for my journey has been plant medicine. Nature has its ways to offer the solutions and medicine that you need when you have made a choice. Living in the forest of Lake Atitlan, Guatemala, I had a friend from Ireland who shared Sacred Geometry ceremonies with cacao. He lived from the heart and was a teacher for me since the first day we met, and little did I know that this encounter would bring me to one of the most powerful experiences in my life.

That night after a six-hour ceremony in which we repeated specifical mantras while looking at sacred geometry, I went to bed and played Lemurian music so I could fall asleep. The moment a high tune vibrated inside my body, I literally felt a crack in my heart. I was shocked, first of all because I didn't even know this was a thing, but when the physical crack happened, I felt a deep expansion of energy from the center of my heart chakra all the way around my body and energy field. This was so new to me, and I believe in that moment that I simply accessed a different state of consciousness or dimension, which I have worked to keep and solidify, more and more. I felt a stronger presence of myself inside the body, and most probably the outside felt it, too. I grew more sensitive but strong, and I had to build stronger and healthier boundaries around me, but at the same time remain open to give and receive.

From this open chakra experience, my whole energy field reached a deeper and larger space, I believe, and I feel like a magnet. My relationship with my own spirituality has taken a whole different course.

Self-Esteem and Love

Opening our heart goes beyond the idea of being open to loving someone and being open to having our hearts broken (which is the story that is feared from this), but you can use this portal, the heart, to generate a great magnetic field that is 5,000 times stronger than the brain. This means that if you are able to unite and create a thought and emotion through repetition, you can have 5,000 times more reach to The Mind.

My beliefs around being vulnerable were an issue of self-esteem. I realized that self-esteem is the deepest form of self-love.

I could love and accept other people, but I would judge myself. This meant that I was not truly loving or accepting others, because there were still parts in myself that I considered negative or shouldn't be there. And, paradoxically, that part of ourselves that is apparently the most negative, is the one that we have to accept and love the most.

By accepting what others criticize about you, it no longer affects you. This means it no longer has power over you.

"The water in which the mystic swims
is the same water a madman drowns in."

— *Joseph Campbell*

The emotions and beliefs on self-esteem reside in the area of the belly, or the third chakra, manipura chakra. They are much more influenced by the illusion of separation and competition. When the heart is closed and the Ego has taken control, we will find it hard to experience pleasure for the success of others, because of not knowing that we are the same expression ourselves as another avatar. Remember that the Ego´s throne sits in the belly, so as long as we are ignorant of being the observer behind the explorer, these emotions of separation and excess individuality can easily be manifested.

There are tools out there that help open the heart, deeply. Here are some examples:

1. Take actions daily toward the life you deserve. In the doing, we direct the emotion.

2. Practice other heart-opening activities: See if you have any sadness, resentment, or unforgiveness that you can start letting go of through unconditional love, compassion, and letting go.

3. Practice giving. Any person that you encounter today, send love to him or her, by visualizing a green light covering their bodies. You can give compliments to animals, plants, and people that you meet, like saying something nice about how they look, or the way in which they are doing something.

4. Practice receiving. Whoever gives you a compliment, receive it. If you receive a gift, receive it and say thank you. Accept what it is given to you, without feeling the need to give it back or feel bad or guilty about receiving it.

If you practice opening your heart, you will enter a different dimension and state of being, and keeping this state until it becomes solid, is also a responsibility that you have to apply to keep your inner environment prone to this state of being.

Love Is a Magnet

Love is the energy from which all is made — it is the highest of living and vibration.

Love is the biggest magnet for positive changes in your life. That is why the things that are passionate for you, the things that you love, will keep your inner fire going infinitely. It all starts within yourself, and as long as you love and accept yourself for who you are, you will start attracting circumstances and people that will reflect your self-love instead of your self- judgment.

Practice being in the heart until it becomes your natural state of being:

1. Journal, and ask yourself what some of the beliefs are around you, opening your heart. Paradoxically speaking, when it is broken, it is also when it is most open. So we can take advantage of this state.

2. Internalize every day the truth that the future that you deserve has already been granted in your heart.

3. Ask yourself how you know whether you're acting from the heart. The first characteristic of being in the heart is the absence of struggle and the presence of ease and simplicity. The heart longs for a natural kind of presence that recognizes and validates itself as an extension of God. The love you give to yourself, others, and the world flows, without getting attached to one specific person, situation, or thing. Real love is not attached to anything: It is a free energy; therefore it is given from the inside to the outside, freely.

4. Ask yourself how you know when you act from ego or fear. Characteristics of being in the ego state are struggles or the need to fight for the things you want. It is competing with someone else's ideas or lifestyles. The heart energy does not exert pressure and is very smooth and gentle by nature.

The thoughts and feelings connected to I want and I need, are connected to the wrong order of things, from the illusion of believing that we need to bring from the outside in.

This will be manifested in the third chakra or solar plexus, like having a black hole that is sucking and pulling everything from the outer to the inner, even energies and things that are not good for us. We then become easily overwhelmed by the world and super influenced and conditioned by it.

117

Once this chakra is in balance, the process then becomes from the in to the out. You will start discerning and using this power to its best when the process changes from out to in, to in to out. Just the experience of living from -in to out- will bring you a deeper sense of union. Because there is a huge difference from wanting to be better from the inside, which will come from self-love, rather than wanting to be better because I am projecting myself with the world and I seem bad, or I should be better, because of the outer world conditioning.

That is why self-love and self-esteem are key. Even if this seems egocentric. There is a fine line between self-love and narcissism, but the more you practice, the easier it'll be when you attach yourself to a profession, to a partner, to a family. All of this will start changing and falling, eventually, since nothing is permanent. And you will start to fall and change along with them. The challenge is, then, to change the order of things: from within to the out.

But how to start working on self-esteem? To know ourselves is to love ourselves. Self-love is the same as our self-esteem. To love ourselves it is important to accept every part of who we are, even parts we have neglected in the past. Even the things we don't like about ourselves.

Choose to love all parts of ourselves, rather than judging them. Through this process, you will start to know your passions, the things that you love the most, based on our self- knowledge. Self-knowledge is based on the complete acceptance of who you are. And it is based on choosing between what unites or what separates.

CHAPTER 10

Sex, Creativity, Money and Healing

Our inner fire — or feminine energy — is waiting to be kindled and directed toward creation, play, exploration, and fun. Our inner fire is also the vital force that is keeping us connected to our bodies and physicality.

Our inner fire, also known as sexual energy, arises from the lower two chakras, our genitalia. It has the capacity to create new life and, basically, anything that we choose. This same energy can be used to create something small and simple, or something as complex and miraculous as a human being with its own heart and mind! It is crazy if we think about it. It is the most powerful energy, because it is the source of human life, of all life.

As active creators, it is important to understand this because we might find ourselves using this energy in ways that don't help us. If we don't know this, and we are disconnected from our bodies, we will live by our instinct and primitive impulses, such as sexual interactions and survival.

Some people live in a constant state of fight or flight, which is also known as stress or survival mode. This is activated by the sympathetic nervous system. The left side of the brain (+), which controls the sympathetic or primitive nervous system, is releasing cortisol and adrenaline in order for the individual to survive, whether you are really in front of a threat or not.

The tricky thing about being in a survival mode or stress mode, is that until you realize that you are, you probably won't notice it. Being stressed has been normalized in our modern society. People usually refer to stress as something that is just there and they have to deal with it because there is nothing to do and because most people are living in stress.

It has been proved that 80% of modern human diseases and sicknesses come from stress.

Some people believe that the way to deal with stress is by using medicinal drugs or opioids, or tobacco, or alcohol. The pharmaceutical industry is seemingly all-powerful. This means that, of course, they would want you to believe that in order to cure stress, you need to take a pill, and that stress is something inevitable because there is no real understanding of it.

It is the lifestyle itself, the food we eat, the neverending rat race for success, the belief of power through money and possessions, the need to pay the huge debt, and a series of behavior that is making people sick because they are simply living in a fear state of consciousness that comes from survival mode, which comes from the continuous release of cortisol and noradrenaline produced by the adrenal glands: a chemical messenger which transmits signals across nerve endings in the body and which is telling you all the time that you need to survive and run for yourself, because there is not enough for all of us! Imagine the amount of energy that your body is constantly releasing by being in survival mode. What first was meant to be creative and fun sexual energy, now has become a signal of continuous fear and need for protection.

The inner fire can be interpreted the same way as we make a campfire. A campfire is kept alive with firewood. The firewood is made of things that we like and the movement of those things like: sharing with our loved ones, having pets, going to the gym, creating, moving our bodies, laughing, and, essentially, experiences that we feel passionate about.

The challenge is that although there are going to be days that we don't feel like doing certain things, as long as we love ourselves, we will know that we deserve our fire to be kept alive. It transcends our humor, it always goes with the certainty of what I deserve. So our every day's work and lifestyle starts turning around to add fuel to work, to our relationships, to our body. Firewood is your passion, it is deciding and not negotiating with yourself if one day you want to add fire or not, it is adding to it despite having a bad day, a sad or bad experience, because one is committed to add fuel to the fire, because it is what I deserve.

So the inner fire is the desire to do better things, essentially, to evolve. The inner flame is self-love, and self-love is held in faith. Because you don't need more reasons to keep this fire alive, but because it feels good, and that is self-love. It is the choosing of keeping it alive, rather than letting it die.

Feeding the Inner Fire

Unless we comprehend our inner fire and how it works, and how to take care of it by being connected to it, it will function to our disadvantage by continuously creating emotions based on fear that will unconsciously force us to make decisions that are far away from our hearts.

Anxiety is familiar to many people who simply accept it as something that's there. But until we realize that we can get out of that state, we will be conditioned by it.

This can lead to be constantly looking for the release of the hormones serotonin and dopamine, which are the hormones that gives us a sensation of happiness and connection, through outside triggers such as sex, drugs, sugary food, and other addictions such as betting, being distracted and using other peoples company just to avoid confronting the void, which only needs to be looked at and filled with love. The void that we are so afraid to feel is actually one of the best things that we can feel, because otherwise there wouldn't be space within for anything new and different. We just have to sit and be present with it, realizing there is nothing to fear because we are the ones meant to fill it simply by being present.

Sex is a very powerful drug. It not only can give us momentary healing and release of accumulated stress in the body, but at the same time if we are continuously releasing energy through orgasms, we will not be directing this beautiful feminine sexual creative energy toward our evolution and towards real creativity.

Breathwork and tantric yoga made me realize the fire inside me, and I started to build a relationship with it. The more I understood how to use my energy, take care of it, the more I learned how to use it toward my goals. If energy is power, then my power is focused. Focused power. I do enjoy sexual interaction, as long as it is healthy and it keeps me balanced, but I have also learned to give to myself what once I received from those sexual encounters, and the more kindled and directed my fire is, I simply become more attractive (magnetic) and the less I need to do in order to create the experiences that I want.

Here are some suggestions for feeling your inner fire:

1. Practice celibacy as if you were practicing fasting. This can help you become aware of your inner fire instead of having sex occasionally, as well with or without a constant partner.

2. Practice pranayama, tantra, or kundalini yoga, which are intentionally created to awaken your inner fire and direct it consciously through your chakras or energy field, with the intention of purifying your channels and chakras, and expanding them.

3. Observe your breath. If you are breathing consciously, you are connected to your body. You are under control of your fire within. Conscious breathing is key to everything else.

4. Breathe slowly and deeply. The slower and deeper your conscious breath is, the slower your heart beats and the slower and deeper the physical processes inside, this means that you can actually rejuvenate your body instead of wearing it out.

5. Understand that the quality of your breath is the quality of your life.

The three lower chakras of the body represent the feminine in the body, which is the creative and emotional one (-). The upper three chakras of the body represent masculine energy, which is vision and direction (+). The inner fire (also known as Kundalini), which resides between the perineum and genitals, will be awakened by will power (taking action) and will be directed through the spine until it reaches the crown. Kundalini or inner fire, like fire itself, will transmute and cleanse everything among the spine, meaning the seven chakras: the technology of your body vessel.

You can start directing your inner fire and building a better relationship with it:

1. Accumulate and build inner fire. By practicing celibacy and/or Pranayama, we will start accumulating inner fire in the lower chakras. Most people will tell you that you need to release your sexual energy by masturbation or sexual interactions.

2. See yourself as a bonfire. Imagine you have 10 logs and you are building a fire. Through practice and knowledge, you will see that you are putting one log at a time so the fire burns slowly and regularly. If you throw all 10 logs into the fire at once, the fire will grow fast and burn quickly, which can be very helpful, as long as you have a clear direction of it. So it depends on you and your capacity of directing this fire by the practice of concentration and focus.

3. Practice with a candle. See what happens if you cover a candle and take away the oxygen. Fire will die. It is showing you that oxygen is needed for the fire to exist, as well as space and direction to grow and expand. The same applies to your body.

4. Direct your fire with intention. Through breathing, direct with your mind and focused imagination, the fire that you are awakening towards your third eye. Hold a vision, that image of what the feeling that you deserve represents for you, and through breathing and creating an emotion, bring it all the way to the third eye, where the vision is being created. Then feel it in your heart and direct the emotionalized vision out from your belly and also down your root chakra, as if you were literally anchoring it on earth.

The relationship you have with your own inner fire, is basically the consciousness of the light and the power of love, learned by you and focused by your mind. It is essentially the knowledge of using it in your favor or intention.

Abundance and Emotional Wealth

To further understand your creative energy, it is important to analyze the concepts of abundance and wealth.

Abundance and wealth are two faces of the same coin, just as with masculine energy and feminine energy. In this case, masculine — the director and the thought — is considered to be structured, so we are going to call this *wealth*, which can be specifically related in the following 4 steps:

Step 1: Time: the human hours of work that you are actually applying into doing something. Let's say this is 6 hours a day or the *time* that will be applied.

Step 2: Knowledge: specific techniques that you know or have about a certain subject. Let's say it is how to do something: a master's degree, a method, a solution to a problem, or essentially any information that gives you tools, the *knowledge* that you can apply with your *time*.

Step 3: Differentiator: your unique essence or what makes you different. If you know what makes you different and unique, then you can use that in creating or doing something different from others. This could be your personality, your perspective, your energy, and essentially the unique combination of talents, passions, gifts, and characteristics that make you who you are.

Step 4: *System*: the combination of time, knowledge and your differentiator, will help you to create a system that will put all of this together, a symbiosis that feeds each other, expanding and giving life to the system itself. Once this becomes an automized system, an extension of who you are outwardly, you have created wealth.

I decided to create an artist's residency program in Lake Atitlán. This answers three main questions when I decide to do something: with whom (my amazing business partners), where (Lake Atitlán), and what (artist residency). Through these programs, people come to this incredible space, create community, create and share art. I can also facilitate yoga and writing retreats, share my work, and basically play and have fun with like-minded people! I have created a system that applies to everything I love and that I'm good at, because I am in love with this lifestyle. My abundance (-) and wealth (+) complement each other.

Before I created this system, I had to do the work and get to know myself, my tools and my resources, and exchange them with people that are benefiting from them. I figured that if I already had a product and service that people liked and were impacted from, why not reach more people?

On the other hand, the feminine energy is more associated with beliefs and emotions. This is what I call abundance. It is important to define it this way because it helps us understand where we need to put the work. Maybe it is in wealth (+), or maybe it is in abundance (-).

So if abundance is a manifestation of my beliefs and emotions around money, and about my capacity to feel abundance and to emotionalize abundance, I will want to know what is the story behind this. For example, do I feel guilty every time I receive or give money? Do I feel like I don't deserve being rich because of the fear around being rejected from my current social environment? Do I fear to stand out and be material of gossip or envy? Or maybe I have a strong belief about money being bad and dirty. If you feel this is where your blockage might be, then what you have to apply now is being able to feel abundant to what you already have.

Gratitude and being abundant are a result of the ability to feel the richness that is already around you.

Even if you want more, you must be able to love and feel gratitude for what you have, or you will miss out on abundance. Being abundant is being capable to see and appreciate the richness in life. There are people who are billionaires who are not abundant. They might be living in a lacking or not enough state still. So it is not about what you have, it is about your capacity to feel it. And naturally, as the laws of mentalism explains, if you feel abundant in spite of your circumstances, you will start attracting more facts to feel abundant.

Serving Others Can Build Wealth

It is essential to know who we are and what we have to offer. The more useful and profitable I become to others, the more I will receive back.

I no longer follow money, but focus on what I am giving. One of the biggest mistakes around the concept of abundance is that we believe that money is what we want. But actually what we really want is the experience and the feeling behind that thing that money will get us.

What is the point of having $1 billion in the bank if I cannot use it? I realized that all I wanted — and what's awaiting me in my future — is about feeling free to do, to create, and to move wherever I want to, whenever I want to, comfortably and safely, and to share art and interesting conversations with people. Yes, money will give me these experiences, but money alone will not, so I decided to focus on the feelings around the experiences rather than on money.

The more impact you have on the world, the more money you will receive. So don't focus on money, but on yourself. Focus on how you can create more value within yourself, through studying or experiencing this and that, by investing in yourself in your personal, emotional, mental, spiritual, and social life, and how you can make yourself better in order to impact better. Because the more value you give out, the more you are going to be receiving.

It is key to understand our relationship and beliefs with money, because the answers are there. And sometimes we believe we want something, but we don´t, so there won't be a union in thought and emotion, but the opposite, because we might not be following our authentic self.

By understanding that I had to stop looking for money, but look for ways to create value in the world and in the system, I knew what my resources, talents, and gifts are, and what I am giving. I am 100% certain that my voice and that my work are super important, because I already have changed one life: my life. And as a life, I am witness to the miracles that I have already created, so if I can impact one life, I can impact millions more.

The word *profit* means a financial gain, especially the difference between the amount earned and the amount spent in buying, operating, or producing something. If we take the word *financial* out of the first sentence, we will have the difference between an amount of energy earned and amount of energy spent. Essentially, if we are being useful and resourceful to others, to the game we are playing, money (a generally accepted unit of exchange in this game reality) will always be coming since we are adding value to it.

That is why, when one is certain, one ceases only to be moved by ambition. Ambition is *a strong desire to do or to achieve something.* But if you already feel the future that awaits you and you are creating value to the game, you are not only moved by a strong desire to achieve something in the future, you are enjoying the present freely.

We can understand this idea as when you jump in your car and you decide you want to go somewhere. Let's say you are in California and you are heading to New York. You will set in your GPS New York, and you will simply drive and know that eventually you are going to arrive at your destination. The GPS tells you that you will arrive in 72 hours, for example, and although you don't yet see the Empire State Building, you know you are going to arrive eventually. There is no desire anymore because you know for a fact that you will be in New York soon, you let it go and enjoy the ride. You already know that your desire is being fulfilled because you are transitioning to get there, so you can either enjoy the ride or watch the clock with impatience — either way, the road takes 72 hours.

But let's say that, since you know you'll get there, you simply enjoy the views, the food on the road, and you'll enjoy your time — you'll laugh, sing, and share. If life throws you a surprise, such as a rock in the middle of the road, an event that can be determined by other causes outside your control, you choose to see the rock as simply getting to New York a few hours or days later, while you enjoy where you are in the present moment, (because maybe you should not arrive that same day). This is your choice on how to perceive that unforeseen scene.

This example can be applied to you knowing that the money or resources that are needed for something that you deserve to experience, is already coming together, whether you see it right now or not. You see? You have replaced the ambition or desire to achieve something that might cause anxiety, stress or impatience, for the one of certainty. Playing with our perspective on things is part of the game. The energy of money has and will always be a neutral energy. It is you who is connecting with it or not, through your beliefs and emotions around it. But once we are open to receiving it with the right motivations, we will jump from a state of looking, lacking, or needing it, into a state of enough and abundance.

Once we enter this state of being, in which we no longer need anything, we will see that it ceases to be important how much money or what kind of position you have, because nobody really cares. Usually the people that do care about this part of your life are people that are worried about you, or are competing with you. And either way, you are not conditioned by them. The important thing is how you use your resources, like your time and your love, your lifestyle, and how you live your life from day to day.

The paradox of this game is the combination of curiosity and certainty of who I am becoming. Being curious on how far do I get in this game and what life is going to give me and the certainty of whatever life throws at you, you'll end up and already are where you decide to be. It is knowing what you have to do today, in order to get there, but at the same time, being open for surprises and challenges to come.

Let's see if it is the abundance of wealth that is blocking you.

1. Discern where in these two things you need balance and reconceptualization. Maybe you need it in both of them, and that is perfect.

2. Practice feeling abundant: feel grateful and satisfied with what you already have. Feel nurtured by what surrounds you on the material, emotional, mental, and spiritual level. Feel and connect with the energy of abundance. Feel and experience already having enough. Abundance is not about being rich — it is about experiencing riches in all that surrounds you.

3. Practice creating wealth: This is something that requires infinite polishing because the more you grow inside, the more you understand things, the more you will be always shifting and perfecting big or small details in your system.

4. Change your own concepts of ambition and certainty, in small or large ways.

If you are in a constant balance between abundance and wealth, you will be able to sustain abundance and wealth. This relationship will make you grow, bloom, and simply experience life the way it was always meant to be experienced: in abundance and flow!

The more you look, the less you get.

1. Stop looking. Start feeling.

2. Understand what is your value in the system. What is it that you can give to the game? In what ways can you create value? Make a list of your resources, talents, and gifts in order to create a system that puts your unique energy out there for others. What are people willing to pay for your unique energy?

3. Believe in yourself; practice certainty.

The more impact you have on others, the more money you will get. We change the order of things, from in to out, rather than from out to in.

1. Think about that if you are able to sell something for 10 people and they love it, why not then not impact 1 million people?

2. Believe and act. Stop procrastinating, if you already know your value, invest, and create a system. This could be a service, a product, etc.

3. Be open to give free services until you create an audience and work constantly into communicating and creating impact for this audience, because the chances that it grows will come from mouth to mouth.

Self-knowledge and belief in our value provide the path to success, and it is our greatest tool of all. By locating ourselves in the game reality as players and explorers, and getting to know our value and our own specific resources, tools, gifts, and talents that are useful to others, it might be easier to understand our own inner economy.

By changing our perspective from wanting money, but asking, 'What are we giving out to the world that is useful and creates solutions to any kind of problem?' the energy of money will start flowing into our lives.

How to Heal Yourself and Others

Our inner fire or sexual, creative energy, is our power to bring something into existence. Whatever that something is, it depends completely on you and your belief system around our creative powers.

We all have the same potential within, whether we pursue it or not, it is no different. We are no different than people out there in the world that have created something incredible like, for example, the technology behind the spaceships, Iphones, or cities. These people simply created solutions to humanity by directing their power into the vision inside their heads. They simply focused their inner fire in expressing into existence what they have already in their minds, through consistent work and believing in themselves and in their vision. Through emotionalizing their vision, and taking action towards it.

The same creative process applies to healing ourselves and others, since the same creative energy is the healing energy. The word heal means to balance. To balance what? Well, the masculine and feminine energies. This idea is important to repeat, since we are those energies already — these energies lie within us and make everything that exists, so thinking that we need something outside in order to balance ourselves, is forgetting and not using our own creative powers.

To understand our healing powers is to understand what unbalances us, too. As explained in the past chapter, as long as there is a fight between the feminine and the masculine energies within us, consciously or unconsciously, unbalance and fight will exist within us, and in the world. The same concept applies here by saying that we can balance ourselves by applying feminine qualities — such as love, warmth, time, care, and movement — in specific parts in our body, as it applies that we can balance ourselves by applying masculine qualities — such as taking physical action, expressing outwardly, placing boundaries — by saying no or yes to certain situations and to act upon our truth.

The chakras in our energy body will manifest the unbalanced energies (emotions), or information, through our physical body. If there is an emotion or information that is stuck and needs to be seen, your body will tell you before it becomes something serious. If everything is energy and we are connected to our bodies, we have the power to balance ourselves before it turns into something serious. This is where food becomes our medicine or our venom. Fruits, vegetables, water, teas, and herbs can help to balance something specifically with their specific qualities.

Since the inner fire is also known as the healing energy, as long as you have a vision that you are healing, the transformation will occur. Remember that having space and time to practice meditation, the universe is giving you a gift and opportunity for self-studying and self- transformation.

Once you start playing and creating, you will only want to become better at it. You just need to create the time and space, and to understand your pace. We are dynamic beings, and life is dynamic. So even if things might feel stuck sometimes, we have the power to add dynamism into what it is under our control.

Here are some tips for adding dynamism when feeling stagnant or low:

1. Take a walk or a shower when feeling stuck.

2. Taking a vacation, or even a small trip somewhere changes our environment and, therefore, our thoughts and feelings. By changing our thinking process, we then change our environment.

3. Put yourself out there. Don't whine about your situation, but become someone with a dynamic attitude, so you can literally bring yourself out of situations that you don't want.

4. In general, try to build dynamism in your days, to create a more enjoyable rhythm in your lifestyle, such as moving your body when feeling stuck in a practice that you enjoy, or finding a creative channel discipline in which you can find clarity within.

Whatever you are going through, there are things you can do to change anything in your life. It is all about will and directed thinking.

The more love we feel, the more we give it freely to ourselves and others, the more we create balance by appreciating the beauty and the love of existence. It is like having a specific lens of love, and expanding this healing energy in every place you go. You then become a healing portal, even if not focused specifically on something, but because the love is flowing through your body and touching everyone around it.

CHAPTER 11

Ancient Wisdom and Modern Life

The Power of Circles for Energy

As above, so below, as within, so without, as the universe, so the soul.

— Hermes Trismegistus

How we perceive and make use of the elements on the outside is how we perceive ourselves on the inside.

The spirit has turned cold for some people. The sparks of life and true love are waiting to be kindled again.

The disconnection to the spirit world and the different beliefs in different cultures and societies have become more of a battle for who is right, rather than simply understanding what this means within ourselves. The spark in ourselves contains the powers and freedom that we have longed for so long.

Some people think spiritual people are passive and boring. I myself have thought and believed that. The best way I can describe my own spirituality now is being on fire and embodied, and focusing it toward creating as I am as active as I have ever been.

It's ok to be in peace and focused. It is being present in love in my human body. It is my duty and responsibility to keep this spark alive and to perceive it as the most sacred thing, that one indestructible, unbeaten, and undefeated part of who I am.

No longer caring about other people's perspectives on my decisions has allowed me to be who I am instead of attempting to live up to external expectations. This is freedom in its maximum expression. Being spiritual is working with supernatural forces, with the Spirit itself, which is the love of God or the love of the Universe, the energy in which everything is held and created.

Practicing my inner powers or magic in circles was where I understood a lot about myself and the power of Mother Earth. Ancient civilizations that are still very active have always worked with the spirit and the elements of Mother Earth. When losing my business and company from the pandemic in 2019, I decided to do something that I always have hoped for: to move to Lake Atitlan, in Guatemala, where I am writing this book, and started to learn about Mayan Cosmology and to apply with more discipline my focused energy sustained by the spirit of Earth. This led me to learn, open my mind and to write about my experiences.

Connect with Your Ancestral Tools

Get out of your comfort zone in order to find different perspectives. I was planning on moving for three months to Lake Atitlan, a beautiful lake in Guatemala where there is a large community of Mayan culture practitioners and Mayan priests. I didn't realize that those three months would turn into my home.

I didn't know that my life was going to change so much, because I found myself surrounded by tools and practices that helped and guided me into knowing who I really am. By living at Lake Atitlan, I had the direct reach for the Mayan and shamanic ancestral knowledge.

If you are interested in connecting more with your ancestrality and ancestral tools, you can start with the following steps:

1. Research of ancestral ceremonies that resonate with you.

2. Read about them or go find them and open your heart to learn from them.

3. Be humble and respectful for their practices, since they are the ones that are carrying and have carried the ancient wisdom towards modern times.

Spirituality is living life sacredly and focused, in surrender and in connection with the Spirit and Mother Earth. I started to attend ceremonies and open my mind and heart for this people's wisdom. I started to study and write about them, and the more I made friends with them, the more they were open to share with me. They could see that my intentions were real, because they were and still are.

How did it happen for me?

1. I was curious and made friends with a Mayan spiritual guide, Walter, who I constantly asked about things. He is still my mentor.

2. I started to understand my relationship with the Spirit of the fire, the cacao, tobacco, and other beings, read the behavior of the fire in the ceremonies, and how it is considered the ear of God for the Mayans, and so the power of our prayers and connection to the fire.

3. I attended my first Mayan fire and psilocybin ancestral prayer ceremony in sacred Mayan altars, which awakened my ancestrality. I learned and experienced that my ancestors live within me, and their energies are present in my earthly body, working with and through me.

Spirituality is being on fire, becoming 24/7 toward our greatest self. If you find spiritual tools and support that resonate with you and that you can apply day to day, you will create a very powerful way of living.

Asking for help is remembering we are children of the Earth and that we are being heard and supported, is having faith in our roots on our birthright to receive when we ask from the heart.

Using Our Minds as Bodies and Bridges

The more we understand our human body technology, as incubators of information that is resonating all the time through emotion — and also as bridges of information from higher sources to this one — the more we can start exploring different states of consciousness and different ways of finding solutions.

Through my ongoing healing process, I have started to connect more deeply with my inner child. Every day I would simply think about my inner child and let her know that she was loved and appreciated, that she was safe and I was with her. I have always been a fan of crystals and stones. I learned that crystals are beings that choose to incarnate on Earth because they hold information and memories within themselves.

They are here to help us to connect with specific information when the time is right. They can also be considered solidified water, and water is a great transmitter of information, such as the emotional body within and outside us. This said, when we are holding tight emotions inside of us, we are becoming denser and denser. This means the energy is stuck, such as a swamp, and the lack of movement will stop new information from coming in.

While living in Lake Atitlán, I was invited to attend a Lemurian meditation that was guided on 22/02/2022. It was a very special date and portal, in which people that were invited would be receiving light codes that would work directly in the emotional body, which could bring new information to the DNA. The way I understood and lived this experience was very intense physically, but also spiritually, because since then, I have become a conscious bridge of information.

The way our body works is incredible, and we are still barely understanding how to actually awaken all its potential. The DNA contains all the information and intelligence within us, but it is is said that only 2% of our DNA has bloomed, and slowly, consciously and unconsciously, we humans have been receiving DNA activation through water we drink, the crystals that are in Earth, and by meditating on the light codes.

While in this Lemurian activation code meditation, I brought my crystals and simply listened to beautiful lemurian chants that were awakening my human awareness from the seeds buried inside me. You can compare this as an alchemical upgrade since our cells vibrate at an increasing rate and our vibratory frequency helps us ascend to higher dimensions, while still very present in the third dimension.

Once the meditation ended, I slept, and I had the most intense dreams in which I literally experienced all the emotions that were still stuck in me. I felt deep sadness, jealousy, treason, and fear at its most intense. I remember I woke up shivering, with my heart beating off my chest, sweating and in shock, not understanding what it was that I had just experienced, until I remembered that I had been into a light code activation meditation the night before. What was happening was that the light codes within me helped me release, while sleeping, the information within me by physically feeling them so they could be finally released from my body.

The months after this meditation, radically changed my life and my plans, and also my sensitivity to higher information. I understood that we are bridges, not only for creation, but also to bring information to this dimension. My body suddenly felt the need to stop smoking weed and tobacco the way I had been doing it, specifically and unconsciously to avoid these feelings that were stuck in my emotional body. Once I stopped smoking weed, I started lucid dreaming again and gained a clearer mind, which helped me focus myself into what I am now writing and understanding about myself.

Communicating Through Crystals

All shamans around the world collect crystals. Crystals have two main purposes upon the Earth: the first and most important is communication with other dimensions, the second one is technology, memory (think that our whole computer industry depends on crystals), we would not have any computers without crystals.

Here are some ways of communicating through crystals:

1. If you feel called to a particular crystal or mineral, research their qualities and what they represent. Most of them are connected to a specific chakra in the body, so you can see if it's your body which is needing a specific energy or seed activation in the DNA that is expressed through this chakra.

2. Meditate and use your crystals during your rituals,

ceremonies, work or healing space, in order to receive that energy and to solidify it within you.

3. Use them for healing and as well for offerings. You can also calibrate a crystal, such as a quartz, with a feeling on your own. Quartz can be neutralized by putting them under earth and on salt water. Then you can program them with an intention or by placing them under the energy of the full or new moon. The information of crystals travels through water bodies, within you and outside you, so you can always expand its energy by placing them inside water containers near your body.

By building a connection and relationship with crystals and the mineral world, we can explore how communication, memory, and technology from crystals can help us through any process we are going through. We ourselves are crystals. So by seeing ourselves through them, we also become aware of being communicators, memory transmitters, and activators, and that we awaken DNA light codes with others. Crystallization, a process that transforms a solution into solid through a controlled process, essentially means to order particles with a defined morphology or form. In this case, this crystallization of information happens within the body.

Here are some tips on how you can start solidifying lighter feelings and states in the physical:

1. Letting go of physical and/or emotional addictions help to be more centered and open to serve the information that could come through you.

2. Drinking lots of water, cacao, instead of caffeine, less consumption of processed food, carbohydrates, red meat, and alcohol helps your body and your vibration to stay high.

3. Surround yourself in expansive and open environments, rather than contractive or stressful ones.

4. Sleeping, preferably in a routine way, not only helps the body to restore and regenerate more deeply, but also through your sleep and dreamworld, you can receive information or make suggestions in the subconscious.

The less attachment to the body, the less suffering there is. Suffering originates from the attachment of the body and the mind, rather than of who we really are. Suffering, therefore, is the denial of what you feel in the body, instead of experiencing what you feel with awareness and acceptance. The human projects himself outside, telling a story of what should be and what shouldn't, and therefore, suffers. By becoming conductors of this feeling, we come out of suffering, and we become creators.

The more you meditate and explore different ways of consciousness, the more you feel familiar with it and the more you can consciously direct yourself into these different states. You can start exploring the dream world by practicing lucid dreaming, as a way of experiencing life from a different state of being and to remember that, as how we dream, we live. The more lucid we are in our dreams, the more lucid we are in this game reality, which is also considered real, simply it is more physical and dense, and, therefore, it is easier to attach to it.

How can I start exploring the dream world?

1. Keep a dream journal.

2. Waking up and writing about your dreams should be the first thing you do every morning before meditation. The more you write down your dreams, the more you are able to remember them.

The more you explore consciously different states of consciousness, the more you awaken different parts of yourself and the better quality of life you can have, from the benefits of the expansion and understanding of your consciousness.

Tools for Self-Knowledge

There are many tools out there that we can support ourselves with, by understanding the meanings of numbers that are always present, or the cycles of the stars.

We can learn about what influences are affecting us, emotionally and psychologically. Astrology and numerology come from the ancient wisdom of Mayans, Greeks, and Egyptians, and from every other ancestral civilization. These tools help bring clarity and information to our soul's purpose. Although they have been considered esoteric sciences that go against mainstream conservative religious beliefs, they are ever-present, whether we believe in them as useful information or not.

Long ago, I started to question everything, and I ended up in a magic school in Guatemala City where I learned a lot about these tools. Numerology resonated the most with me, because it seemed like a very practical tool. My association with numbers had always been math, and since I was not very passionate about these topics at school and university, my relationship with numbers was very superficial. Another tool that resonated with me was the Tarot and the reading of Akashic records, and as I still explore the different lines and influences, astral planes and dimensions, I bring better understanding about the essence behind this material or mental tools.

It was through the combination of Pitagoric Numerology, the seven laws of the Universe of Hermes, and the seven chakras based in my Yoga knowledge, that I started to see the link between those three within the body, and I started to understand how I could balance myself and use these energies in my path. I naturally started making readings on other people, finding the patterns, and helping them understand how they could balance themselves by simply understanding the information within each chakra, and not only to balance, but to actually use more actively the law of the wisdom related to the dominant chakra in their bodies.

People loved it, and I started to become more obsessed about it, until I decided that I would create a book about it since people who found valuable information in my sessions could take something with them that they could support themselves whenever they needed it. That is why I wrote my first nonfiction book, The Free Will Method, which includes a chart where people can read and understand themselves better through the combination of these three tools. It is essentially, to make a better use of one's energy and talents, and to focus them accurately. It is wisdom applied in practice.

Sharing your process to others helps you deepen your understanding about the particular moment you are going through, but also you can help people to upbring that understanding within. Remember we talked about understanding things so we can actually apply them? Well, I find this very accurate when applying it to myself. I found this through Numerology, since I could define and confirm that my solar plexus is my dominant chakra, from which I process information and also I had to work on my self-esteem and expressive masculine energy.

Taking change and decisions seriously is an act of self-love and will take us towards the future that we deserve. No one says it is easy. It is infinite inner polishing and perfecting ourselves, one thought at a time. Whether it is through this channel or the other, it doesn't really make a difference, as long as it serves a purpose of bringing solutions to humanity — healing and balancing suffering, all should be accepted and applied as powerful tools that are helping to create a better world.

Master Plants that Support Us

Recent scientific medical studies have shown that there are long-term benefits of experiencing Master Plants in a responsible way.

The *setting* and the *set* are vital keys for the individual to have a good experience with these master plants. These experiences can be life-changing, since they shift our sense of self. *Setting* meaning the place and space where you do it, and whom you are doing it with, and *set* meaning your headspace and mindset. You should definitely want to have this experience as long as you are completely sure about it, and it is you who is making the decision, not someone else *for* you.

Although there has been increasing interest around these experiences, I would deeply suggest having your experience led by elders who traditionally can teach and share about the plant and the ceremony. It is not supposed to be recreational. If it isn't treated properly, it can have counterproductive effects.

I explored *ayahuasca* to understand and heal some of my deepest wounds. I entered a different world, which my soul already knew existed, and simply rested from being in my body, which was very unbalanced emotionally. I had all these burdens and *samskaras,* a yogic term for the imprints of our past actions that condition our present moment.

I felt the energy of love pouring and filling all of these imprints in my psyche and liberating me from them. I experienced so much relief in that moment, that a lot of things came out of my body from this relief and relaxation.

I used to have a hard time communicating my feelings with others because I just didn't feel safe expressing myself and simply didn't have the clarity to express my very intense feelings and emotions. That is why I decided to write, because it was my safe space, and I realized that through scuba diving, I was already being taken care of because I was called to connect with my emotional self, which needed healing. I had already started my Yoga journey while scuba diving, even if I wasn't aware of it, and that had prepared me to make the decision of exploring different states of consciousness.

The name *ayahuasca* originates in the Quechua language, where *aya* means soul or ancestors, and *wasca* (huasca) means vine or rope. This is referred to as a master plant, *"The Grandmother,"* connected to the spirit of feminine energy, or the home energy which, although each experience is undefinable, can help to bring compassion, love, acceptance and connection to Home, since it represents the energy of the *Am* and brings healing to the connection to the mother.

Peyote, a cactus native to Mexico and southern parts of the United States, contains mescaline and is associated with the spirit of masculine energy, or the energy of the I. Again, like any other Master Plants, it is hard to describe since it usually brings to the individual the experience that the individual needs. Peyote helps to ground, to focus, to discern, to bring vision, bring confidence to one's dreams, to believe in oneself and brings energy to the connection to the father.

Magic mushrooms, from mushrooms containing *psilocybin*, were used in ceremonial practices thanks to Maria Sabina, a Mexican oaxaca shaman who helped heal people with it. Psilocybin is connected to the energy of joy, lightness, and a childlike spirit, and helps neuropsychiatric conditions. It also enhances energy, memory, compassion, love; it creates a deeper connection to one's heart and brings healing to the inner child.

Huachuma, a quechua word for the Andean plant medicine

commonly known as *San Pedro cactus*, is said to be a key that opens the gates of heaven. It contains the same psychoactive hallucinogenic ingredient (mescaline) as peyote. Known as *"The Grandfather,"* it is helpful for people with post-traumatic stress disorder, or personal issues that require a gentler approach.

I believed that if I wanted to know who I was, I should trust the medicine of plants to start with. The information for creation is encoded in nature, rather than in pharmaceuticals, so if someone is looking for deep and long-term healing from trauma or ancestral pain, plant medicine has the cure for every burden and hurt. Clarity, discernment, developed psychic abilities, love for your body and life, forgiveness, and others, are some of the benefits you can bring out of these experiences.

Sometimes what scares us most, is what will set us free. I was questioning my beliefs around master plants and finding out for myself. You can start by asking yourself the following questions:

1. What do you truly know about master plants?

2. Research scientific studies concerning master plants or psychedelics, and how they can help heal diseases or conditions that modern medicines can't when used correctly and under the right supervision.

3. Try it out for yourself.

If nature's wisdom is infinite and all that there is, why are we not trusting it?

CHAPTER 12

Fiction, Nonfiction and Magic in Our Lives

Although believing in magic is often considered silly or crazy, a living part within us recognizes our human potential when we watch heroes and fantastical beings doing fantastical and great things.

I believe that hope is a slowly awakening potential that is deeply identified with what we see in some magical movies. We might still not recognize this as something within us but mostly as something that occurs in non-human worlds where only a few beings have these superpowers. In the same way, we can see fantastical characters as having human qualities, such as nobility, honesty, courage, love, partnership, passion, challenges, emotions, frustrations, fears, etc.

We identify with these fictional characters through their emotions, even if they themselves seem far from our natures. We can change our perspective by engaging with books and films that use concepts of magic, such as the Harry Potter or Lord of the Rings films.

Some years ago, I made a promise to myself that I would believe and live through the dimension of magic. In writing my novel *The Game of Crystals*, I expressed my process. Although it is a novel, it is related to my biographical journey. I felt like a true alchemist since I was literally working with my stories and turning them into gold.

Gold itself, as a rare metal with unusual properties, a conductor of heat and electricity, is also malleable and ductile. It's a symbol of immortality, because it has long represented the Sun in many cultures (just as silver represents the Moon). Gold's rarity (and inert properties) made it a prized possession for kings and nobles, and, until very recently, it was the prime medium of exchange in most monetary systems. Ancient alchemy, as seen in fiction novels and movies, goes beyond the essence of chemistry, which is based on trying to find a way to change nonprecious metals into gold. Ancient alchemy says that man is the base metal that is refined and perfected by the process of psychotherapy (the condition of moods and feelings, thoughts and behaviors). This means the reprogramming of the mindset, meaning that we are meant to become gold ourselves.

Hermes Trismegisto, the Greek version of the ibis-headed Egyptian moon god Thoth is considered the patron saint of alchemists. *"That which is above is like that which is below: and that which is below is like that which is above to accomplish the miracles of one thing"* are the cryptic watchwords of alchemical transmutation that establish the correspondence between the universe (the macrocosm or The Mind, the **AM** (-)) and man (the microcosm or the mind, the **I** (+)). So as long as we are capable of transmuting our emotions and stories into wisdom, we are applying the essence of true ancient alchemy. All men are potentially gold, for gold is the intention of nature with regard to all men.

Even Sir Isaac Newton (1642-1727), one of the greatest scientific geniuses of all time, said: *"Man must finish the work which Nature has left incomplete."* I interpret this as becoming who we really are and who we really are intended to become, based on the cards that were dealt to us.

Finding the Tools for Creating Our Magic

How do we find the tools and courage to create our alchemical magic so we become gold in ourselves?

Any circumstance is an opportunity for us to do the work. There is no specific place to go, there is no need to move to this place or another. If you think you need to go somewhere or achieve something to get to the truth, why not find it now and here? It can be found in anything, if you really are open and use your imagination, the magic and the potentiality of alchemy will reveal itself to you 24/7, *everywhere*.

I now learn from the magic in all of these movies about magic and apply it to my life. For example, I recall the *Patronus* spell from Harry Potter, when any thought of fear is hunting me. To use the *patronus*, I think about the happiest moment in my life. This dissolves the energy of fear. Fiction and fantastical movies have become a primary source of information for my creative process, because I am becoming magical myself through engaging with the heroic and fantastical qualities that are represented by these fantastic characters, the ones that I believe I have and are taking place within me and within the world.

This was my experience through writing fiction, which changed my relationship with fiction itself:

1. I understood the Hero's Journey concept expressed by Joseph Campbell. I then studied the line of narration behind the stories that I loved the most, such as in *The Lord of the Rings*, and associated that with my own life.

2. Writing my own Hero´s Journey based on my life and a particular experience I wanted to write and share with the world in my book *The Game of Crystals* gave me the chance to redefine my past. It was not fiction for me — it was simply seeing myself through different characters and redefining my experiences.

3. I experienced my story from different perspectives and characters, so I lost identification with my own character, and I redefined my past.

4. Apply the *Expecto Patronum* in your life. Whenever you feel in doubt or in fear, bring the best memory you have and awaken the love and change the fear from focusing on this memory and observe how your body and perspective changes.

5. Another Harry Potter spell was the *Riddikulus* spell — by visualizing your biggest fear as something funny, so instead of

growing serious inside, you laugh at your fear.

So how can we start practicing putting in action our own story, instead of the ones that we have heard from other people? How can we start using our imagination? Suggestions:

1. Redefine/replace existing definitions on fiction or nonfiction, fantastical or real, because such definitions can automatically condition/restrict your perspective.

2. Imagine your life as a fantasy movie. You are the hero and the main character, as well as the screenplay writer and the director and producer. What new adventures will your main character experience to get to that ending that is already written? How can each experience that is sent from life be transmuted into the creation of this amazing future?

3. Imagination is one of the most powerful tools for creation. It all starts there, in your third eye or mind, activated by the right side of the brain (-). So working and practicing imagination is key to creating, because you need to see it in your mind first, without the interruption of *how, when, or this is not possible.*

If you are able to disassociate from your life and imagine a movie about it, you can create some connections, discover patterns, and get to know yourself from a different perspective and use this knowledge towards your goals. That is why consuming fiction or fantastic content can bring wisdom to your life, not only by giving us a different perspective on ourselves and on the game reality, but also how we are experiencing this experience, which is the narrative behind our experiences: our story.

How Symbols Helps Us Understand Our Power

Through fiction we can understand certain symbols. As I write this, I am on the banks of Lake Atitlan in Guatemala, looking toward the hill of gold, Cerro de Oro, the hill where author Antoine de Saint-Exupéry was inspired when he wrote *The Little Prince.*

Seeing with the heart, as the Little Prince did, is a feeling and a way of life. Legends around Lake Atitlan are plenty. One speaks about dragons. Three dragons are the guardians of the lake. Two, who are twins — one male, one female — live underwater and the third, the grandmother of the other two dragons, lives in Santiago Lagoon, which is surrounded by three volcanoes, which guard over a crystal temple inside the lagoon. About a year ago, I found a piece of quartz in San Marcos, one of the 12 towns that surround Lake Atitlan, and I bought it immediately because it had the form of a dragon inside.

I started to dream about entering a dragon egg and a voice in my dream said: *She is already in.* I felt it was kind of an initiation. I had another intense dream about entering a white room where a dragon was. I was invisible and small, but the dragon could perceive me and was close to eating me a couple of times. I felt that I was scuba diving, but I was flying and floating in the white room. My mission was to kill the dragon, before it killed me. So I managed to guide the dragon´s head all the way underneath its own belly, between its feet, and from there, the dragon launched fire and killed himself. Once it was dead, some of my friends whom the dragon had eaten escaped its belly alive, with a gold liquid on their bodies.

I feel a connection to dragons now, and as I know that most probably I won't see one or touch one with my physical body, I know they exist in other dimensions, and I know that they are present in my life for a reason. That is why I believe that watching movies or reading novels (fiction, of course) on dragons can reveal important information.

Fiction allows writers to use their imagination. The symbols, places, and characters help and support the author and the reader to contextualize, enrich, and comprehend something that cannot be explained.

Using All Your Senses

The Mayan *nawal* (energy) linked to the dragon is *Kan*, the energy that represents the natural flow of things, the internal fire that begins in the spine and extends to the rest of the body (also known as *Kundalini*).

Kan is symbolized by the serpent, the dragon, or Quetzoalcoatl (the flying snake) which represents evolution in all its forms. It represents DNA activation, justice, truth, instinct, intuition, intelligence, and peace. It is the symbol of fire and passion, and energy that encourages the finding of passion and taking the risks to develop strength and power. It is a sign that you are on your way to a big spiritual and powerful awakening or transformation. It is a bold and aggressive energy that urges us to use our powers of healing and better ourselves physically, emotionally, and spiritually.

This information that flows within me, and the experiences that I live in this and other dimensions, give me great content for my books. There is an important reason behind why I am documenting this.

It is only with the heart that one can see rightly;
what is essential is invisible to the eye.

— *The Little Prince, by Antoine de Saint-Exupéry*

Reality can be experienced as a game reality. Everything is energy, in a constant vibration. Reality is not really experienced only with the senses, but it is experienced through the heart.

Let's explore this idea through the following:

1. Ask yourself, what are you feeling now? If you are somewhere specifically, can you train yourself to perceive what is not visible to the eye? What is what you are feeling in your heart?

2. Can you ask yourself, what do your favorite mythological creatures represent? Maybe it is not that you are going to see them physically, but you can feel and understand symbolically what they represent. It could be courage, faith, boldness, transfor- mation, or strength of heart.

3. Ask yourself, what spirit animal represents you at this moment? Do you feel a deep connection to birds, to water animals, felines, or reptiles? Can you see that these prototypes are awakening certain things inside? What are they?

If essentials are invisible to the eye and we practice different perceptions, we will open ourselves to different dimensions and energies. Researching and understanding what you feel, rather than what is pure fact, will bring you answers such as in a common pattern or interest in content that you are consuming in this moment, because most probably it means something.

I feel a deep connection to dragons and what they represent. I'm writing about them in my new novel, *333 Grid*. Signals in my dreams are telling me something that can be helpful and bring more awareness into what the universe is reflecting. I opened my mind and asked the following questions:

1. Is the energy of dragons trying to tell me something? Why do I continuously keep on seeing and finding information and signals about them?

2. I asked if they could reveal this information in my dreams. And so it happened, in one dream which was very vivid during a full moon, I saw myself as a little girl walking inside of the egg of a dragon and someone whispered: *She is finally in.* I still don't know what this means exactly, but I know that I will know when I am ready to know.

3. Staying open to synchronicities has brought people in my life with the same interest in dragons. Now that it is common for me. I also realized in the Chinese Horoscope that I am a dragon, so I just keep on researching this symbolism through my curiosity and awareness.

Through my own practice of magic and astral traveling practices, my inner fire or magic power was fed the more I talked about these subjects. I had faith that I would be taken to magical places and situations that would eventually bring me the understanding that I was ready to receive.

The Strength to Leap into the Unknown

Taking a leap of faith allows you to open your heart and mind.

The concept of the *fool* in Tarot represents innocence, naïveté, not knowing — because you already know it in your heart, in your essence. It is your willingness to get out of the cave, to the unknown, to fall and make mistakes, because maybe you will define everything that happens to you as an adventure. It is taking the chains off, inviting others to join, and making a way to a different world.

Once you understand and know this, it is hard to stop, and it is impossible to go back. You will be called a fool, misfit, outcast, and crazy. But deep inside you will know that staring at the wall of the cave is an illusion that can no longer hold you down.

Here are some suggestions for learning from other people to gain the strength you need:

1. Write down the names of people who you look after or think about for information.

2. Read biographies and follow people who have initiated something in the history of time in any situation. It could be Jesus, Einstein, Plato, Socrates, Tesla, Hermes or anyone who is inspirational and who can help you create a solid mindset.

3. Ask yourself (and journal) — What do these characters have in common? What did they choose to do about it?

Other people's beliefs about you should not be taken personally. So stepping out of the personal importance, and simply committing to playing the game, will lead you to what you already know is true, because it can even sound crazy to you! If you accept and laugh at the idea that you will sound crazy, then you can start having fun with it.

What are you doing about it?

1. Ask yourself, Are you the one judging yourself? Remember that life is a self-fulfilling prophecy. If you think it's crazy, it is crazy. If you think it is possible, it is possible. Whatever you think you can or cannot do, you are right.

2. Choose certainty over doubt, over and over again.

3. Stop saying," I don't have enough money to create this" or "I don't know how to do this." Change your narrative. Start saying: "I will find a way" or "solutions are coming."

4. Stop asking for hows or whens. Stay open. Start asking, "What can I do today and in this moment to help the process along?"

5. Once you understand the creative process, the idea is to have

fun with your creations. It is not about the creation itself, but about the process and about you as the creator.

Here are some suggestions on how to start to create like crazy:

Higher-self meditation:

- Think bigger, think bolder. There are no limits but the one that you choose. The idea is to find a dream that is limitless, because you will always be growing towards becoming the person or the self that is creating this limitless dream.

- Don't be afraid to dream big. You can always start by journaling this 100 times higher dream and keep it to yourself — you don't always have to involve more people in the beginning.

- Describe the qualities of your *Atman* (soul). Feel it now, be thankful, be certain, and let it become your new state of being.

- Think about your dream or project as a newborn child. It needs some time to nurture in the first stages until it becomes an infant and can actually go out to school and think for itself. Protect and nurture your new idea in the beginning, such as you would protect your newborn child.

Find inspiration through different characters in history, in their specific time frame, and see how these inevitable personalities have come to resolve the waters of that time, and how by them believing in themselves, have left steps that allow other things to happen. These small or big, but powerful, acts of love, have honored our inner potential, their essence, and, therefore, they have already changed the course of humanity, they have created a different reality simply by being themselves and tapping into their own magical powers.

CHAPTER 13

Human Emotions and Power

Theories about the creation of Earth vary, and at the same time tell the same story. Such tales express the idea of human emotion from its origins and how emotions can either limit us while at the same time provide us with our greatest power. It depends on our perspective and knowledge toward them.

This is a great time to build a better relationship with our emotions. If we are not balanced emotionally, we are subjects of manipulation, because we are constantly being pulled and triggered into thinking, and therefore acting, a certain way through our emotions. As long as we are unaware of this, we are going to believe that we are choosing what we are doing, even though we are not.

Emotions can refer to information that creates what we define as anger or happiness. These frequencies travel through the water inside of your body and affect moods, thinking processes, decision-making, habits, and a series of choices in life.

Some people think that emotions are our enemies because they seem to control us and have power over us. This is true, as long as we ignore how to use them to our favor.

As long as you are controlling your thinking, you control your emotions. A good way to explain this is that whenever you feel sad or bored or frustrated, you have two choices. You can choose to stay where you are, feeling helpless and accepting this mood or emotion as something you must live with, or you can move from where you are, and take yourself out of the emotion. Some emotions can be challenging, but as information they tell us something about our thinking and what we are experiencing.

Every specific piece of information, concentrated in the hormonal glands or chakras, responds to the outer world. We associate with the world outside through memory or repetition patterns in the brain, which create stimuli or reactions. Through his theory of classical conditioning, the Russian physiologist Ivan Pavlov explained the idea of how we can be conditioned by emotions and, therefore, how we can change them. He proved that consistent and repetitive learning (which leads to a reaction through memory) creates a conditioned response through associations between an unconditioned stimulus and a neutral stimulus.

Think about the taste of the lemon and feel it in your mouth. You can experience the sensation of acidity that a lemon creates in your body, even without actually biting into it. The same thing happens when we feel aroused or excited by thinking about someone we desire, or we feel sad when we watch a movie, or think about someone we loved and lost.

As long as we are unaware of what is being triggered inside of us, and why and what is triggering it, we will constantly be acting and making decisions based on those triggers. Marketing professionals understand that to sell a product they will have more success if the way they market their product creates a reaction in the consumer that triggers an emotion — happiness, fun, success, fear, peace.

You can stop reacting to the outer world. You can actually decide and create new associations that are actually valuable to the life that you deserve, and start making different decisions that will result in true happiness. If you don't master your emotions, you risk being manipulated into taking decisions not necessarily for your higher good. The pharma industry, the media, and the government know this very well.

You can master your emotions by learning from experience,

becoming wise about what emotions serve you, what emotions are just conditioned patterns, to create a healthier filter between your inner and your outer world. Before the outer information triggers something inside, you will already have changed your belief and association with what it is triggering.

Legends of Civilization and Emotions

When planet Earth was created, it was the perfect place for the incubation of energies. Planet Earth was the place where a lot of light beings came to experience the different landscapes, to explore creative processes and to reproduce. They came to experience physicality and creation. But along with light beings came dark ones. Dark beings need to live and exist through the light of others because they cannot produce their own. They are not stars, like us. Planet Earth was the place known as Eden.

The fall of Atlantis and patterns in the culture can help understand how and why we have been controlled by emotions, but also how we can use our free will from real freedom, a power that was meant for humans to forget since it is the way to get us out of slavery.

Humans went through a devolution when Atlantis sank around 30,000 years ago. The fall of Atlantis is the fall of insensitivity to the environment. Beings could create at the speed of thought, but we got so involved with the creation that we forgot our spirit legacy and who we were. We became the creation. We got lost in the game.

We can get that power back by accepting the dimension of magic. This is best known by the indigenous societies who were the first to exist in a state of awe. They simply dealt with what was in front of them. Our modern Judeo-Christian culture suppressed the indigenous empires. The spirit of the individual was denigrated, and people were taught that the way to power — false power — was through groups. By seeking acceptance at any price, people became disconnected from themselves. Civilization created people who have no self. They create a group identity. They don't commune in nature by themselves, they don't have original thoughts, they don't evaluate the information by themselves, because they are distracted in competing and surviving.

On the other hand, in ancient Egypt, humans worshiped the aspects of the divine yet to be discovered. That was how ancient Egypt worked — the culture was designed to help humans become gods. We used to know as a fact that we were born as humans, with the intention of becoming gods. To discover the aspects of the divine by looking always for something within, a path towards I AM. For example, if you wanted to know what is the light, you would question the light until you understood you are the light. What is the darkness? Question the darkness until you understand you are the darkness. You question everything, until you question, Who I am? I am the tree, I am the light, I am the darkness. I am that I am.

Lately, we are in the path of going back again to those practices, untangling slowly from becoming accepted on a human common group level just to feel connected to anything, and it is easier to buy into all the propaganda.

- Ask yourself, do you feel the most connected by yourself or with others? Have you ever felt your truth doesn't align completely to everyone else's?

Reptilians brought to humanity all the information of survival.

As humans, three dimensional beings, we have to experience death, unlike eternal beings in the 4th and 5th dimensions. That is why we experience survival. Reptilians taught us how to survive and how to pass information among blood to other beings through codes of emotion in our DNA. Reptilians used emotion to capture and to awaken the power of information. Reptilians were the first beings to experience survival and learned how to be eternal, even to exist in death.

That is why reptilians and emotions have a deep connection. Cold-blooded, they can control the energy of their bodies, when to shut it up or turn it on, something that the mammals cannot do. They were builders of wisdom on this planet. That is why all the gods and goddesses of history at first were snakes, or related to snakes; all regions in the planet like Kundalini in India, dragons in the Mediterranean sea, in China, Japan; the God snake in México, in all North America, the sacred snake of the Amazonia, and every snake in Egypt that we can see reflected in the heads of the kings and queens. Snakes were the most important beings for us because they gave us knowledge: the information of how to rule ourselves, and everything that we could possibly understand on this planet. That is why snakes became a symbol of enlightenment.

- Ask yourself and journal, what have you heard about snakes, or what do they represent for you?

- In whatever culture you were born in, or grew up in, what was the belief system around snakes?

That is why from the very beginning in history for all humans, women were God. Women were an extension of the creator. They were able to create life, because in order to create, you need a lot of emotion. You cannot create without emotions because you need a lot of energy to create life. Women have lots of energy, lots of emotions. This energy had to be aligned with the spiritual process to connect with the goddess. And this energy has the spin shape of a snake throughout the body.

Reptilians taught women how to create life and how to handle men on Earth, so they could understand how to create a society ruled by the emotion of women and by the wisdom of the creator. So women became the first priestesses, the first shamans of history to understand how everything worked. To understand that the universe had the shape of a tree, so they learned about this tree that has all the information, and the fruits of the tree is all the wisdom that we can achieve in our lives. So every culture had this sacred tree and the snake that teaches women how to handle that information.

When the Annunaki came after the Reptilians, they wanted to rule differently. They settled in Persia and started to create the new order of civilization. They took the power of the reptilians and started to rule the planet through their wisdom. Men started to take control of society, and that made the reptilians and women taken for the same thing. That is why we have now Christianity expressing that the snake ruled the women and that is why we are a mess today.

Our modern system is ruled by the concept of survival — it is the reptilian brain talking every time we think: *I need to survive, I need to fight, I need to eat.* The alchemists held this information, learned by the Masons in the Middle East, and they brought it to Europe. And then, with the rebirth of Science and Arts, the Illuminati took that information again. So the rulers of the New World Order took the same information that Reptilians used to have in the history of humanity. So that is why our system is ruled by the concept of survival: through emotions.

Sometimes, understanding where our present and fear-based systems come from can bring us clarity of who we are. The research on past beings or different theories about our connection to energy, the universe and wisdom, can help us understand how powerful we are and all of the influences that have passed and are still here, and the reason for it.

The Battle for Power

Although surviving is key, of course, and it is a basic and primitive part of who we are, we are more than just survivors. We are meant to love and to experience the gifts of creation, we are a representation of God within a water body, so considering us simply survivalists is a waste of our potentiality.

By developing our concept of free will, we can start to direct it toward exploring who we are, creating societies and new inventions, different ways of doing something, to create ourselves as who we imagine and feel we are.

Ignoring who we are has made us manipulatable through emotions, and we continue to choose to serve others instead of ourselves, or simply to serve our real purpose. Our human potential and specific skills brought many energies down to Earth, which made us believe different stories about ourselves and about God and the Universe. Beings that came from the skies considered themselves Gods and learned that they could control humans through fear. They said that if humans didn't behave or believed a certain way, they would be punished through storms, earthquakes, drought, etc. They made humans believe that free will was choosing between doing what was right and what was wrong under the eyes of this new belief system. They "took" our power away by making us forget our essence and controlled us through fear through a system that, until today, still remains.

Being connected to our hearts and our own truth will set us

free. Keeping faith and hope in change for humanity will create the change. But how do we start to create change? As long as you have consciousness of what you are creating through your thoughts and emotions, change won't be hard to follow.

Our past selves have created the present moment. The present moment has been created by a combination of things, but mostly from fear-based or ego-state consciousness. So as long as you have the consciousness that you are creating through your emotions, and you are creating different vibration frequencies such as love, peace, and joy, even if it's far from what you are looking and hearing all the time in the news and media, even if the planet seems to be falling apart with so many disasters, as long as you are anchoring a new reality through your body, and not fear, you are already creating a new future for humanity.

It is vital to let go of heavy and dense emotions such as fear, anger, rage, hopelessness, and frustration that block us from feeling lighter. We create what we feel.

The denser we are, the more susceptible we are to manipulation and disconnection with our lighter being and Atman (our soul). It comes back to being responsible for our lives and our actions. So if we come back to the main message of this book, which is connecting to your power, embodying into your avatar, and making use of it by directing it consciously into a vision of yourself — the lighter you feel and are, the clearer you will see.

- To see clearer, practice pranayama or breathwork, since it will expand your life source or light, helping to release trapped emotions (blocked energy in the body) and therefore, balance it and bring clarity.

- Eat lighter foods. Food itself has different element compositions, from solidity to liquidity. Fasting therefore helps, because the body will start eating the debris in the body when you are fasting, and by eating itself, the information that might be stuck in the body, will be released.

- Practice discernment. How could you know if an emotion is heavy or light for you? Heaviness brings blurriness, fogginess, and tiredness. Lightness brings clarity and vitality.

So can you think of a time when you felt the need to act, but couldn't think straight because your body was already pulling you to do something? What did you do? And, what could you do? If you speed down your heartbeat to neutrality, then you will see that you can simply think better when there are no emotions asking for you to survive or react. Take your time.

- Practice disassociation of emotion. As talked about in the past chapters, changing the story around an emotion will eventually stop having power over you.

Looking for lightness is key to knowing your light. If you are constantly on the path to feel less and less heavy through food and emotions, you will feel the difference and will become prone to anchor a higher frequency in your body. This will bring clarity in your life, as well as a less prone body system to be controlled by emotions.

CHAPTER 14

Solutions in Other Dimensions

Portals on Earth to Different Dimensions

There are specific places on Earth that retain and sustain, or incubate, a specific vibration.

These are the emotions of the Earth. Earth itself has its own chakra or technological system. The root chakra, muladhara, is found in Mount Shasta, California; the sacral chakra, svadhisthana, is found in Lake Titicaca, Perú and Bolivia. The manipura chakra, the solar plexus, is found in Uluru and Kata Tjuta, Australia. The heart chakra or anahata, is found in Stonehenge, Glastonbury, Somerset, Dorset and Shaftesbury, United Kingdom. The throat chakra or vishudha is found in the Giza pyramid, Egypt. The third eye or Ajna chakra is a moving chakra, and the crown chakra or Sahasrara is found in Mount Kailash, in Himalayan Tibet.

There are other very energetic and highly vibrational places on Earth, such as the Pacific Ocean and other water bodies, caves, and Lake Atitlán, for example. The seven main energetic places are portals that emanate a specific vibration. People from around the world, with or without this knowledge, can be drawn to specific places in order to download information that has been seeded in the DNA. We contain all the information within, and intuitively we can feel deeply drawn somewhere,

163

even if we don´t know why. Usually it is for this reason, because a program in a specific place is looking to be awakened within you, or you intentionally can go places in order to awaken something within.

Ancestral civilizations have practiced opening portals without the need to physically move. They can be opened in specific times of the year due to astrological and astronomical events information, such as equinoxes or solstices, or some dates such as the 22/02/2022 or 08/08/2024. Portals essentially mean a door that opens, and sometimes this door can only be appreciated and is revealed to the beings that hold a specific vibration. If there is a body that holds very dense vibration, it will be too dense (due to stuck emotions in the body) probably to actually feel and become sentient of this lighter vibration.

I have experienced being present in portals and have been guided by intuition to portals in Peru and other places. Time and space feel different there, the connection is stronger and feels more, therefore we can use it to create. Once there is a connection to our own bodies, it is easier to listen to the inner compass. It is easier to trust and to feel the guidance from the heart.

In Peru, I asked Mother Earth for guidance. I wished to experience a ceremony of Huachuma, a master plant local to Peru. I was guided to the ceremony and to different portals around the Sacred Valley by an Inca shaman. Finally, we arrived at the most magical places of all: to the heart of Pachamama, a portal, that I understood my prayers had been listened to by my mother, to be nurtured, held and listened to. I was going through a hard time and through my prayers, she took care of me.

I also understood that, like the Earth, our bodies are portals as well, and our heart is the most powerful door, the space in the body where time and space don't exist, because it is time and space itself. And by activating and aligning our human technology, we can create energy portals.

This specific journey to Pachamama's heart portal gave me a profound certainty of the existence of my own portal inside, and the real and deep connection from my heart to Earth. I confirmed something very important to me, and took another leap of faith, which is being bolder into believing who I am and empowering myself in the journey of my heart, and the knowing that I am being guided and held all the time.

Usually, there are places where there has been a lot of prayer or energy involved, or they can be natural places related to the North and South Pole and the Kundalini of Earth in which energy concentrates differently. I believe I am in Lake Atitlan, Guatemala, right now, because I am supposed to be doing what I am doing. Some people ask me, How do you manage to do everything that you are doing? Writing books, managing a business, creating new projects, facilitating retreats, and making time to travel and enjoy? I just say that being here makes me relaxed so I can actually focus on what I know I need to do. Ideas and inspiration come fast, and every day I experience magic because I am open and believe in it, so everyday I have plenty of material to work with. I feel like being here elevates my vibration, so everything I say becomes a reality faster than in other places. If I were living in a big city, for example, maybe it would be more challenging for me to focus on doing just what's really important. In nature, the collective belief system field that would attack my magical beliefs is nonexistent; therefore, I don't have to be struggling with those kinds of thoughts and resistance all the time.

How can you bring better understanding about portals?

1. Research or think about places on Planet Earth where you would want to visit. Is there any specific feeling or reason you feel called to go to a country or place? Is it a cave, a temple, pyramids, or a city?

2. Ask yourself, 'Do I feel called to go or visit a water body or a place surrounded or near a water body?' Or maybe you are called to go to the mountains, and be more connected to the earth? Or maybe to the height of a volcano?

3. Journal about the ideal place in your mind. Usually, there is a magical and ideal place in our mind, where we feel comfortable, safe, and completely ourselves. It is a place surrounded by elements like water, fire, earth, or air, or all of them.

Ask for guidance and help, and explore with medicinal plants. When you ask with faith, you will receive.

Ask for Guidance for Other Dimensions

I went to Cusco, Peru, en route to a retreat planned in Bogota, Colombia. I had always wanted to visit Peru. I ended up there at a moment in my life when I needed to be there, because I was having a hard time dealing with a break-up and most of my plans had fallen apart. I felt naked, empty, and I felt that anything could happen, because I didn't know what would happen.

When arriving with tears in my eyes, the only thing I had left was my mother, Mother Earth, my prayer, and my heart. That is how I felt.

Every day I found a place where I could connect with her, sitting on the ground and meditating. I would close my meditations asking for guidance, asking for her to feel me in those lands, asking her for comfort and guidance because I felt completely lost.

In Machu Picchu, I asked a guard to let me meditate for at least 20 minutes, alone in an intimate space, even though I knew it was illegal. But there were so many people in Machu Picchu that it would be almost impossible to actually meditate deeply. The guard saw that my intentions were real and took me to a closed garden in the temple where I meditated for 20 minutes.

After my five-day trek to Machu Picchu, I explored the sacred valley, spending two nights in Ollantaytambo, where I met two women who had spent four months there. They were about to leave for Cusco, while I was heading to Pizac. I decided to visit a friend on the way to Pizac, from Ollantaytambo.

I had been looking for a Huachuma ceremony, using a master plant that grows in Peru, but I hoped to experience it with an Inca shaman, not just anybody that would do it. I asked my friend who told me it would be difficult to find someone authentic, so I let it go and walked back to the road to catch a bus to Pizac, when a van stopped in front of me just as I came to the street. It was perfect timing, one minute before or after would have changed this destiny. In the van, the two women from the bed and breakfast asked me if I needed a ride and I said, Yes, of course! They were going to Pizac, same as me!

In the car, we started talking, and one of them was a medicine woman who invited me to a Huachuma ceremony the next day in Cusco! I couldn´t believe it, but I realized it was Mother Earth that had guided me there to them, and I was about to experience something incredible the next day!

How to ask for help when feeling stagnant, lost, or any other reason:

- When feeling lost or not, ask for help! Always ask Mother Earth, by touching it, walking barefoot on it, offering flowers, sugar, and offering your menstrual blood or crystals to it.

- Remember you are a child of Earth, you are part of nature, a creation of it, and your birthright is to receive all of the blessings and abundance from all that is. We forget this, and then we don't even know how to ask, or we feel we don't deserve to ask.

- Reconnect with your roots and with the place you are in. This creates a great relationship between yourself and the world. This can make you realize how sustained you are and that everything that you want when you ask for, you will receive.

- You are a portal, so by keeping your heart open and balanced, by nurturing it with love, compassion, and giving and receiving compliments and love from others, the information you need will flow there, as well as guidance, solutions, and love.

You already have everything inside your heart. Of course, if traveling is something that you love, you should do it, but your heart is already everywhere and in every time. You have the greatest portal located inside your heart, and you, yourself, are a living and moving portal. You can travel anywhere and whenever, without the need to physically move anywhere, but by your mind and your heart.

Solutions in Hypnosis

Part of my spiritual journey has been receiving hypnosis and trusting what I was channeling while I was reading tarot to other people, or while meditating. While studying akashic records with a group of people, we started practicing our psychic abilities, and I suddenly found myself bringing information to a complete stranger, which confirmed what I was seeing in my visions. The more I practiced this specific type of meditation, the more I started to channel messages for other people and for myself, and I healed emotionally and physically.

Practice your magic:

- Practice your psychic abilities with metals. Inside a piece of paper, put a metallic object and close it down. Place 4 other pieces of paper in small balls and place them all together inside an empty cup and then throw them on top of a nonmetal table or floor. Close your eyes and place your hand on top of each one of them and start feeling the metal inside the piece of paper until you start trusting your sensory perception with your hand, which sometimes can come up in our minds as a vision, too.

- Remember, these abilities are not foreign or alienated — they are part of who you are. There is nothing strange or new about practicing this because it is part of who we are: high sensory beings with different bodies that we might just ignore or feel disconnected from.

- Don't judge what you like or feel drawn to. Remember, it is about expressing love and building opportunities to grow from love. Whatever path or channel you take, it is not as important as the awareness behind it.

By exploring these different aspects of ourselves, we can shift our perception of the self. Plato expressed through his *Theory of Forms* that what we see in the material world as a form, is merely mimicking the real, *underlying form*.

The alpha state of mind — the one that is accessed through meditation, the one that is just before going into deep dreaming — is the perfect state to self-suggest and to receive information from height information. This state activates the parasympathetic nervous system, which releases melatonin and, therefore, the mind and body enters a sleeping state, releasing impulses in the body for the actual restoration and regeneration of the organs to take place. This state can be induced also by meditation, called deep relaxation or hypnosis. The mental cycles that we experience, here, will induce the body to a different state, and can reach a state like the one we experience in our dreams.

The more you practice being in the alpha state of mind, the more you can do it consciously. You can ask questions, you can visualize your body completely healed, you can ask for healing someone else, you can visualize whatever you are creating, and the seed in the subconscious will be seeded more efficiently.

By understanding alpha, beta, delta, and other consciousness states, it is also to understand that there is not just one state of consciousness that exists — it is our consciousness that is free to explore itself through different states. Once we understand we are not our bodies only, but we are multidimensional beings in this game reality, which is also held from different strings of space/time or dimensions. The more present we can be in those realms, the more present we can be in the physical one, the game reality, the more we are going to understand our own relation with The Mind.

So by exploring these different states of consciousness, our association with the Self or The Mind changes; it brings a more real idea of what this game reality really is, but, more importantly, about who you really are.

CHAPTER 15

The Evidence of My Magical Life

How My Wounds Fed My Power

The resignification of my past transformed my wounds into my biggest power.

For a long time I believed I was a victim, and I thought that would last my entire life. But I learned that I can change. I know that If I hadn't had the experiences that forged me and forced me to look for understanding, I probably wouldn't have become the person that I am today. I am at peace with feeling what needs to be felt. Some wounds take a longer time to heal, and that is okay, too.

I now have great tools that I have earned through my exploration. I have wisdom, certainty, and self-knowledge. To become who I am, I had to make a series of decisions that took me to face my shadow and my biggest fears. I feel proud of who I am because I think I chose the hard way, the path that is not usually taken, the path of the heart.

Yoga has been the path that has helped and guided me. How yoga came into my life shows how the worst things that happen to us can become our greatest gifts. In my teenage years, I was all about sports and fitness. I was very active, playing lots of sports, mostly soccer, horseback riding, and tennis. It was in one of the soccer games that I was deeply wounded on my left knee; my meniscus and the ligaments around it were completely injured. I underwent rehabilitation for eight months. The second time this happened, my doctor told me I could no longer play soccer. I had 10 months of rehabilitation. The doctor said, if you play again, I would need surgery and a longer rehabilitation. I was in deep physical pain. I couldn't go out with my friends, drive my car, or do most of my favorite things. That is how I started to practice yoga, which not only healed my knee, but, like the Theory of Forms of Plato, gave me access to a whole new world: the world inside my own mind.

Since a Young age I started questioning many things due to a series of situations that broke my innocence. I was prematurely and suddenly navigating feelings of guilt, confusion and uncomfortableness. I grew with a belief that I couldn't trust anyone and I justified my actions and my faults with the story of being a victim, as if that was actually helping me or the world.

I decided to stop playing victim and to step back into my power. Actually, no one was able to take my innocence and power away from me, as long as I didn't allow it. My experiences with plant medicines and inner child meditation helped me a lot in this journey. It was not an easy process, but once I let go of fear and emotions and really started to heal the relationship with my inner child, the relationships I had with others in the world healed, as well. I finally had the clarity to look back and give a different meaning to what had happened. I thought that, if that amazing future I deserve is there, waiting for me, I then had to have the experiences in the past in order to grow and understand who I was.

My wounds have now become my allies and my biggest power. I am even grateful, because I had discovered a treasure from what first seemed something pitiful. I became who I am today: free and powerful.

What role are you going to play?

- Decide whether things will simply happen to you, or you create them.

- Ask yourself, if you created this moment, what are you

creating for the future now? How are you experiencing this experience, whatever *this* could be? Are you justifying your wounds and allowing them to stop you?

- Get out of victim mode, even if you got hurt in the past, and it is a complete tragedy. Getting out of victim mode is stepping back into your power again, even if it's hard.

Take Charge of Your Life

As Nelson Madela said, "Our biggest fear is that we are powerful beyond measure." We should stop taking things personally, even if they seem or appear super personal, and decide to take charge of our life.

Even if it goes against our nature, we might find more comfort in staying small, because of the fear of standing out, than to awaken and direct our power. This is scary. I have experienced it personally because this can mean we are going to expose other people's mediocre mind programming as well. But, again, that is their choice, and if they are ready, instead of playing small, they, too, will start stepping back into their own power. I realized that choosing to step back into my power would probably lose people around me, which made me sad and scared at the same time. But then I thought that it would probably also take me to people who would celebrate and liberate me even more. That is what I really deserved. Pause, for a moment — can you let this sink in?

Nelson Mandela also explained this idea, originally expressed by Marianne Williamson, in his most famous speech:

"We were born to manifest the glory of God that is within us.
It is not just in some of us, it is for everyone. And as we let our own light
shine, we give other people permission to do the same.
As we are liberated from our own fear,
our presence automatically liberates others."

Let's analyze your relationship with your infinite power through the following questions:

- Ask yourself, in what areas of your life are you shrinking yourself in order to not feel inadequate?

- Ask yourself, are some of these decisions of not standing out come from fear of not belonging? In your family maybe? In your community? In your own country? Among your closest friends?

- Ask yourself, 'What favor am I doing other people by choosing this way? And on the opposite hand, what favor am I doing to other people by showing my light to them?'

To be responsible is also to express who you are. Without fear, without limit, to be who you are completely, to embrace yourself completely, to love yourself completely. You are the hero in the hero's journey. Let's analyze ourselves through the lens of Joseph Campbell's twelve Hero's Journey stages:

1. The first step is what we know as *The Ordinary World*. This is where we meet our inner Hero and identify with him or her. The Hero is likely known to his or her circle as ordinary. This is the very beginning of the story.

2. The second step is known as *The Call to Adventure*. This is when a challenge is presented to the Hero, a challenge to come out of his or her shelter, like a conflict, event, or a problem that asks for Adventure. This could be anything that simply interrupts the ordinary flow of an ordinary day and is asking you to make a decision.

3. The third step is the *Refusal of the Call*. The Hero initially rejects this call because of fear. Perhaps your family will be disappointed in you taking action, your boss will not like you leaving your work, or maybe you are afraid of change and the unknown.

4. The fourth step is known as *Meeting the Mentor*. The mentor is the person who helps you, the Hero, gain confidence to continue. The mentor believes in you and advises you to overcome your fears.

5. The fifth step is *Crossing the Threshold*. Once you have decided to go on the adventure, you are also open to the unknown challenges that this might bring you. Outside your personal shell, anything can happen, for good or for bad. It is time for you to pack your things and leave your known world.

6. The sixth step is *Tests, Allies, Enemies*. Outside your personal shell, you have to learn who you need to trust. Sometimes we learn who to trust through experiences with the wrong people and being disappointed. And sometimes we just know deeply who can help us, which could be any friend in your life that you meet or comes with you through your Adventure, supporting you with resources that complement your own.

7. The seventh step is the *Approach to the Innermost Cave*. These are the moments where you start facing the challenges that will bring your fears to the surface, but also your inner resources. Think about when you have come out of your comfort zone and been challenged by the world, but by going through the dark cave or transcending our fears, you have now become stronger and a more courageous Hero.

8. The eighth step is *The Ordeal*. This is the most difficult challenge. It could mean leaving the familiar world behind or letting go of a relationship. It could mean losing everything that you have, which requires you to delve deep into yourself to address your most significant challenge. This promises the greatest of all rewards: your freedom.

9. The ninth step is known as *The Hero overcame the greatest fear and challenge to earn the reward*. Once you trust and overcome the challenge, your true self and true resources are revealed. The reward is much higher than what initially the Hero thought it was. The experience has transformed the Hero and has brought wisdom and true alchemy into his or her life. Think about the freedom that you have received when releasing fears by living your truth.

10. The tenth step is known as *The Road Back*. This stage is when the Hero accepts to come back to the ordinary world. He or she has changed, but the adventure has been completed, and you are ready to return home. This can mean a resistance to go back because your old world seems so far away now. But by accepting coming back, it is also accepting to share what you have attained through your adventure.

11. The eleventh step is *The Resurrection*. This is the climax of the story. It is a final test that pops out on the way back home. It

might be a last challenge to prove the Hero's wisdom and the asking of solidification of the new state of being. This could mean death for the Hero, and the Hero is tempted to look back into his or her past and choose. This is the moment where the Hero faces the deep, dark secret that will bring the biggest of the rewards.

12. The twelfth step is the *Return with the Elixir*. This is the final reward after the hero was resurrected and has returned to the ordinary world. There are no more reasons for the Hero to go back to his old habits, which are limited and ordinary. Now the hero is extraordinary because he knows himself or herself and their own powers. With the help of your allies, you now go back home with the elixir and share it with your community.

To see yourself as a Hero inside a Hero's journey structure can help you define and clarify your story. You step out and you step into your story, you are free to define your past experiences and also to surrender the path that is already taking you to your amazing future. Remember that the greatest story of all is that of your own life. Your life is what you want to create out of it. You are the creator of your life. You are what you create with yourself.

Death as Life

When attaching to a personality or a story, we then limit our possibilities of change. Think about a time when you have deeply believed you are someone based on your status quo, on the partner that is with you, on your job or position (all of them changeable and volatile things).

Even if these beliefs about who you are can be deeply rooted in your psyche — that doesn't mean they are true, they are just simply stories that create a personality or Ego. The personality is the characteristic patterns of thoughts, feelings and behaviors that make a person unique. The personality also means: *a personal reality*. So essentially, the reality that you live is a reflection of your persona. Your persona is based on a name, an age, a last name, and basically who you think you are.

But deep inside, we are more than our thoughts, feelings, and

176

behaviors. Essentially our personality has been forged due to our past experiences, religious and cultural beliefs, memories, future projections, and more. It has just become a normality to believe that we are our personality, and sometimes we create this personality in order to survive.

For example, I, a Guatemalan woman who realized that she was attracted to women instead of men, broke the persona I thought I was when growing up. I wasn´t the Cindy who people thought I was, and who I thought I was. And although I was very scared to be turned down because I was different, I could have chosen to pretend to be someone I was not. Instead, I chose to be who I felt I was.

The first thing I did when I got to Indonesia in 2016, just before my trip to India, was to shave my head, because I knew and intended to kill my character, which no longer resonated with who I really was. I needed to reinvent myself, go naked through my darkness, and decided to call myself by a different name: *Loba* (she-wolf).

It seemed like the spirit of the wolves were with me during my trip to India, because they appeared to me through visions, feelings, and people. One of my best friends and a person that inspired me greatly in my trip was *Charlie Wolf*, a very magnetic and powerful Australian yogi. She revealed a world for me that I ignored, because she saw my inner potential that was awakening within me, before even I did. I became Loba, a nongender explorer, an alchemist, and, as an outcome, a goddess.

My intention of being open and surrendering brought me to experience so many incredible, hard, and fun situations that felt part of a deeper experience by itself. It was in Rishikesh, while hanging out with *Charlie Wolf*, where I met a very interesting Italian traveler who was on his way to become a monk in Tibet. He shared with me a Tibetan meditation called: *The demon meditation*.

I didn't know what he was talking about when he invited me to do that meditation with him, but I did know that I had to go to India to work and heal my shadow, the darkness that kept conditioning my decisions. I was very curious, but at the same time I was scared, and I asked him to explain to me what this meant. He said that demons could become our biggest allies, if we only learned what they were feeding themselves on from us (just like the Dementors in Harry

Potter movies), essentially if we got to know what they really wanted.

He explained to me that in order to see them and take our power back from them, we would have to know them, and so we started the meditation. In my novel, *The Game of Crystals*, I narrate this meditation through the main character's journey into a dark cave, where she is asked if she wants to transcend the matter, even if it will cost her life. She says yes and literally faces her fears, her demons, one by one.

In meditation, the first demon I encountered was the fear of death. It literally told me that he was feeding off my fear of dying. I illustrate this demon in my novel as the illusion of death, where the main character is forced to walk into fire. The second one was the demon feeding off my fear of knowing myself and my power, my confidence. I illustrate this demon in the novel as jumping and swimming under a water cave without knowing where she is headed, or even if there was even a way out. She decides to trust her intuition and her body and the current of the underwater movement inside of her that leads her way. The third demon was my codependency with people, and this was the clearest one for me because I experienced the encounter of the demon again in my dreams that night, after the meditation ended.

The death of these demons that were feeding on me, through the fear of death, of distrust in myself and my codependency on others, have been an ongoing process. But to work with them, I needed to know they were there. This has brought me to who I am now, to the freedom of choosing who I want to be, not by fearing who I am not. This is freedom. I am who I decide to be.

Who You Are and Who You Are Not

Getting to know yourself is getting to know who you are not.

I have tried to be this and that, until I realized I just had to be myself. But to be myself, I had to kill who I was not. This is part of the process of becoming.

Death is a way of living:

1. Ask yourself and journal, 'Have there been times in my life

when I wanted to belong and, therefore, I pretended I was something I was not?' Can you not judge this, but on the opposite side, see the trail of becoming who you really are?

2. Finding a space and time to get to know yourself, is actually a decision of killing something you are not, or in other words, killing the false ego.

3. Read the *Tibetan Book of the Dead* to understand, in a deeper way, how your relationship with death can help you live a better and more fulfilling life.

The concept of dying and living is something worth researching as well, since it brings a sense of lightness around death, since we are always dying, we are always changing, we are always awakening. If you are open to die, to let yourself die, you will create space for the birth of your Atman (soul), your real and higher self.

Bring in the Light

Once light is brought to darkness, the darkness dissolves. Once you look at your shadow, it stops hunting you. Once you make peace with those parts of yourself that you don't necessarily like or you are scared of seeing, that darkness ceases to feed from your light and inner fire. You then become a more unified being, with more energy in favor, and less conditioning from the unknown.

It was not until I decided to go to India to face my darkness using the tools of yoga, meditation, and the sacred mountains of the Himalayas, that I actually healed my wounds.

I decided to sit with myself and let my inner world reveal itself while I would accept it, understand it, and start to love and heal it. Until I actually faced it consciously, it would always be conditioning my life. And so I did, it was then that I started to awaken joy back into my life, the reason why I wrote my second novel, *The Game of Crystals*, as a reminder that even though we can go through the most challenging experiences while being innocent, as long as we don´t forget who we are, we can always play, apply our magic, alchemize, and work with our stories, restore our connection with our hearts, and actually use our wounds to become whole again.

The characters of my novel were real characters that I met in my journey, and the feeling that I felt is the one that is told in my story. Most of the scenes that I wrote really happened to me, especially the process in which I felt secure back into my body and started to crystalize my consciousness within my body. I promised myself that I would never forget to play again and that I would keep my heart open.

By applying reverse engineering to my past, seeing from my future and higher self backwards, understanding that my past experiences are creating my future and that this is a game reality that I am exploring -- all this made me feel grateful for my past and my present. I am a very active player in this reality game and already have created amazing things for myself and others. And whenever something hard or challenging comes into my way, I remember it is all a game, which gives me a more playful and lighter perspective.

By changing the way I perceived my story, I changed the meaning of my story. Since I already know that I am heading toward this amazing future that I always see in my mind and feel in my heart, when I looked back to my wounds and pains, I decided that these experiences were forging myself and putting myself into the path that I am walking.

Here are some suggestions for using your darkness and wounds as your allies:

1. Apply reverse engineering from the future that is waiting for you, look back from the final outcome (the feeling that you deserve to feel) and understand that everything that happened to you and is happening to you, is because it's taking you there.

2. Create your own journey and bring the dots together. I wrote *The Game of Crystals* to integrate my own *Hero´s Journey* process and share the elixir or the juice of my process to the world. I thought that if this process would become something beautiful such as a novel and a movie or TV series, then my story could inspire not only myself more, but others, as well.

3. By sharing the elixir of my story, I completed the Hero's journey, created closure, and created new beginnings and possibilities in my story.

4. I let go.

Integrate and share in whatever way possible is part of the hero's journey. It also solidifies the learning within you, because the wisdom that you found, the gold that you discovered from your experience, can now be used by others. This made me let go of my past and my future. Integration led to deep gratitude, therefore, I let go completely.

How to let go completely of a past version of yourself from a place of love:

1. Let go of the story by disassociating yourself from it. Disassociate yourself with the character who experienced the experience completely, so you can know who you really are. And then experience the experience differently.

2. Be grateful for your decisions, your courage, and your path.

3. Think about how your story has already helped you? Has it made you more humble? More wise? More sensitive? More empathetic? Can you see above the fear, pain, and anger?

When sharing, you are solidifying the knowledge of your experiences. Feeling lighter and being committed to releasing emotional blockages in your body, helps you to see clearly and to empower yourself in your path.

I understood and applied the power of recognition. *Stopping to look for recognition outside was the best thing I could give myself*. All I needed was to recognize myself, and a wave of power flooded from my soul to my avatar.

How to become an active player of this game reality we call life:

1. Stop looking and expecting recognition on the outside. Ultimately, stop perceiving life just from your external outputs (your physical senses), and start perceiving it from your heart and intuition. This will grant you the greatest freedom and power of all.

2. Decide to see yourself as you long for someone else to see you. If you really recognize yourself as who you really are, you integrate something great within you. It is like bringing the

pieces of a puzzle back together. It is giving yourself what you expect for others (the outer world) to give to you.

3. If you recognize yourself as who you really are, there is nothing else really left to do. You have cracked the game.

By hacking the game reality, you have arrived home. You have arrived back to the ocean and let the ocean be, through you. You can stay there, if you choose. It has always been your oldest and only real home. You stop needing anything anymore, you have become free and wise. You have become one hell of an explorer, the captain of your amazing vessel, the visionary and the creator. You exist in different places, but you are deeply anchored and connected to your body.

You have started incarnating your full capacity within your human technology.

CHAPTER 16

Embody your Ego

Choose What You Deserve

Unless we stop and use our willpower to decide that we no longer want self-doubt, to live in fear, to live small, and to change our limiting beliefs into higher truths, we will be foreigners of our powers. We will be strangers to our capacity of creating something out of what it seems, nothing. We will not experience the dimension of magic.

The moment that my life seemed to fall apart, when the plans that I so deeply wanted simply vanished from my near future, I entered a state of depression and confusion.

I had done everything right with my ex-partner, whom I dreamed of living with in Mexico City and building an amazing writer's life together. I didn't have a north and direction, which was driving me crazy. Where did I want to go? What was I going to do? Even though I knew I had to trust and be guided, the pain and sadness were real, and I wished for clarity. I had to be patient while months passed by and I still didn't know how or where I would be moving. I no longer had a job, only my books and my wisdom, and I no longer had a home. I was living in my parents' house. This frustrated me deeply, but I decided that I could actually use this opportunity, where nothing seemed to be moving or happening for me. I was inspired by the creation process from the book, *The Free Will Method*.

So three times a day or more, every single day, I would meditate and talk as if I would already be living the life of my dreams. My mother would call me crazy and weird — because who spends that much time meditating when there is a need to look for work and make money and find answers? I knew she wouldn't understand that I was doing all that with my mind, so I simply kept on trusting myself and my method.

I spent my time reading, researching, and applying what I thought could serve me. I did rituals on the Earth, I journaled and looked for inspiration, even though there seemed to be none. I knew that I had to apply my knowledge into action, especially if I was selling a method for manifestors. I had to be my own best client and prove it by myself.

You choose what you believe you deserve, you incorporate, you incarnate: This is the process of becoming. I then made a choice. I would think about the future that I deserved without thinking about no one else but me. This was new and interesting because for the last few years I had been thinking about my partner and me. I printed pictures of my future house, drew some dynamics inside the house, my meditation spot, my exercise spot, my dog, my library, my amazing job directing a whole section in an amazing and successful editorial house. I imagined myself writing and directing a group of people into producing books and screenplay writings for movies and TV series. I felt super healthy, sexy, strong, and complete.

I had made a choice, and now I was incorporating that choice. I became that new person, visualizing and feeling how my books would sell around the world and how they might impact people, making them believe in themselves and building a magical life for themselves. I became a different person. And, thus, created a different reality for myself.

Here is how I support myself and keep my inner fire and inspiration flowing:

1. I read books that inspire me: documentaries, biographies, and personal growth authors.

2. I worked daily on my mindset — beliefs, dominant thoughts, perspective, vision, and emotions.

3. I made a choice and committed myself to it. I decided I was going to create a life for myself.

I was building the life of my dreams. I knew that if I could nurture the seed, the universe would help me achieve it in its own mysterious ways. In the following steps, we are going to apply *The Free Will Method*:

1. <u>Make a choice of what you want</u>. Write your vision or intention, write a date when it's going to be done, and write the feelings that surround this intention. Change your beliefs around this intention since you know that It's vital that you believe you can make this happen. If you apply action with faith, you become unstoppable.

2. <u>Incorporate</u>. Integrate in the body in meditation by believing that you already have it and by being and living the feeling outcome of the decision you want to experience.

3. <u>Feed the fire</u>: Use your imagination. Imagine your thoughts becoming energy inside your body, and the more time and attention you spend sustaining this thought, the stronger it becomes and the denser it becomes in your body until it becomes an emotion and a feeling. It becomes physical. Once it anchors in the body or the physical reality, then it will manifest back as a creation.

4. <u>Practice every day, whenever you can</u>. This will create a continuous expansion of the feeling through your energetic field. Do this daily, out loud and with a clear vision in your mind.

5. <u>Incarnate</u>. Incarnation is key to creating something since incorporation needs to be sustained. To incarnate means to put in the body, to put in the flesh, so your incorporation state becomes your new state of being. It is no longer something that you do for 30 minutes a day, it is the person that you have created to be and you are that person 24/7.

To create a routine or a lifestyle around the creation process, it is the highest level of creation. You are no longer creating just something, you are creating yourself and your whole life.

People follow methods because they have proved to others that they work towards a specific thing or goal. I invite you to polish a method that can help you, as long as it is working for you.

The Right Environment for Your New Self

"The spiritual is the life, the mental Is the builder, the physical Is the result."

— Edgar Cayce

Using my willpower to remain focused into the amazing future that is already awaiting for me, comes down to one thing: being certain of that.

Experiencing this shift, this deep knowing of where I am heading, has given me a great understanding of how to create and how to sustain this creative process from a place of love, surrender, and presence. This is the wisdom that I need in order to walk towards my amazing future, the continuous polishing of myself, the same way warriors strengthen themselves during battle.

Once you have created that future for yourself, that new state of consciousness of knowing, it is vital for you to solidify and sustain this new state of being. You can find a methodical way in which to sustain and create a sustainable environment in order for this state to actually coexist and crystallize within you. Essentially it is not something that you experience once and you create from this state once, but you actually become this new state. From this state, there is nothing else happening, but you, being.

There are different methods that you can support yourself with, such as *The Free Will Method* or *The Silva Method*.

The truest way I can explain this new state of being is to the process of incarnation of my higher self into the third dimension, because I am literally existing in a different multidimensional, and, paradoxically, more physical experience. That is why I believe the physical reality comes closer to a simulation reality, and the realest reality is the one that I am feeling and seeing through my third eye or highest vision, independently and unconditionally from what the physical reality is showing.

The more we know our mind and start to build from it, the more fun and creative we become. Sharing my process with others gives me great value, because I believe that if more free people are using their power with their highest being, a better place and quality life for humanity, in balance with the ecosystem, can be created.

There is a lot of information about manifestation and creation. I invest time understanding what I am really passionate about. Understanding how my brain works and understanding that I like to perceive the world in a rationalized way so I can actually learn how to apply knowledge in my life, has made me realize that I should read and research as much as I can until I actually discover the right formula for me.

Here is how to commit yourself now:

1. Make a commitment to yourself: You are going to hack the game.

2. Invest time and money in learning, practicing and confirming what works for you and what doesn't.

3. By applying and practicing *The Free Will Method*, you can create a link between the body and chakras, Numerology, and the Laws of the universe, which can help you understand where specifically in your body and emotions you can help yourself with.

If the body avatar is the incubator of the emotion, I needed to understand how the incubation works and where in the body it would be needed to apply balance and work the specific law of the universe connected to it.

The laws of the Universe are metaphysical, the branch of philosophy that deals with the first principles of things, including abstract concepts such as being, knowing, substance, cause, identity, time, and space. I figured that if I put them in practice, I would be working with the energies of this universe, or God.

Studying and putting in practice the law of the universe can give you a deeper understanding and weave yourself and your dreams around a web that has the wisdom of creation. The whole world and universe lies within us, so we can also find the expression of these laws in our chakras or energy vortexes, and through our own individual algorithm, we can practically apply them.

Nothing Can Stop Us

Becoming our higher selves involves putting in action and letting our inner potential come to life in the physical, by living, anchoring, and experiencing it through our physical bodies. It's the transformation and materialization that is proving something that has always existed, we are just physicalizing it and experiencing it in a different way, showing others that they can do it as well. It is bringing the higher dimensions into the third dimension. It is essentially the understanding behind this dimension that needs to happen in this dimension. In order to ascend to the higher dimensions, you need to descend first, in other words: the physicalization of the higher self takes place, because you are your higher self already. Your soul reaches down to the muladhara chakra, and up to the crown chakra, coming back to the center of your avatar: to your heart.

If you are ready to overcome any fear of being magical and powerful, to be courageous and to take that leap of faith into the unknown (away from the cave), regarding what costs you, your *powerful you* is waiting for you. Deciding to be powerful and certain, it is a decision you need to make every day at every time:

1. Solidifying the feeling of certainty through practice and through building self references on small things that I have manifested already.

2. I was surprised that I was literally manifesting what I was aiming for, and then I realized that the next step was to cultivate the feeling and not let it go away. That is why I am writing this book, so not only does my process stay documented, but it can also help other people to tap into their magical and creative powers by applying the knowledge that helped me. But also, by writing and wiring ideas together from my mind, my mind is reading and solidifying these ideas

again, on the inside.

3. Meditating every day to sustain a meditation state, meaning the following: sustaining the state of being from the heart, from the future, from the present, all existing at once here and now.

Everything comes from deciding. Decision-making is a habit. This is something that is needed to reiterate because it is the most important thing. You are the only one choosing how to perceive the world. Now, here in this moment, you are choosing if you believe in yourself and in your creative power. This was my process:

1. I trusted my feelings rather than what I was seeing and perceiving with my senses.

2. I meditated and experienced feeling complete just because I can and I rather do that than not do it.

3. I made different choices, from a higher place, from a more loving space, from my higher self. What and how would my higher self see, act, think and decide?

4. I found peace in my present by accepting it completely and continuously letting go of my future.

5. I started to talk to people about this, my voice became stronger and more solid, I grew more confident and I understood that this power was within me.

To solidify an internal mindset that can be practiced every day, every time, and can also be explained and expressed externally so other people can benefit from it as well. Remember that the end of the hero's journey process is to come back home and share the elixir or the juice of our experiences. We are not only helping others through our own experiences, but we are solidifying something within ourselves. We become wise.

How can you close your cycle?

- Choose to spend time alone or in a space in nature that offers the opportunity for your new self to bloom.

- Remember that the established system has sold us the story that we need this and that in order to be complete and free, in order to be validated and recognized. But understanding that you are always going to be exposed to the opposite or different from what you want and who you are, you can choose to embrace yourself more and more, by rooting yourself more into your soul and into your story.

- Recognize yourself all the time. You are the observer behind the explorer, and you are the explorer. You are already everything that you always have dreamed of being. It is simply a process in which this higher self embodies down to the physical, to the ego.

- Share your own story through your own channel so you can see and understand deeper the patterns, the paths, and the vision with more clarity.

This is the wisdom that leads you to paradise. Wisdom will take you anywhere you want. You have always been your higher self, and maybe it's time for you to recognize this part within you. If you are already everything that you have dreamed of, an all-creator, then you just simply have to allow its embodiment to take place, by healing your physical body and by visualizing and accepting your power.

By allowing this to take place, we are bringing parts of us together, integrating, from what was separated once. We consciously become multidimensional beings, being every aspect of who we are, together and in existence in this space and time.

We are honoring who we are: the light and the ocean itself, experiencing an ego.

ABOUT THE AUTHOR

Cindy Barascout is a writer, yoga, and meditation instructor.

At the age of 21, Cindy's life took a transformative turn when she discovered her passion for yoga. This ignited a four-year odyssey into the depths of Tantra Yoga, followed by rigorous training in Hatha Vinyasa and Rocket Yoga.

Today, Cindy calls the enchanting shores of Lake Atitlán in Guatemala home. Here, she seamlessly weaves her love for yoga, meditation, and the written word. She is the author of "Your Free Will" and "Embody Your Ego", two insightful guides to self-discovery and personal growth.

Cindy is also a novelist. In 2017 she penned "The Book That Saved the Seas," a thought-provoking narrative unraveling the complex world of the mysteries under the ocean, its politics and economic game, interwoven with the enigmatic existence of mermaids. She released her second novel, "The Game of Crystals," in July 2021 to great acclaim.

Beyond her creative pursuits, Cindy instructs writer's retreats on Lake Atitlán, helping aspiring authors explore their authentic voices. Cindy Barascout remains a beacon of inspiration in the world of yoga, literature, and cultural exchange.